MODELING AND PAINTING

VIETNAM WARGAMES

MICHAEL FARNWORTH

Published by Military Miniature Press
militaryminiaturepress.com

Paperback Edition, 2022

Designer: Kevin Opp
Illustrator: Tiffany Petitt
Map Illustrators: Julia Lillo and Rocío Espín

Publisher's Cataloging-in-Publication data

Names: Farnworth, Michael, author.
Title: Modeling and Painting Vietnam Wargames/
Michael Farnworth.
Description: Gettysburg, PA: Military Miniature Press, 2022.
Identifiers: ISBN 9781737442615 (paperback) |
9781737442622 (epub) | 9781737442639 (pdf)
Subjects: LCSH Military miniatures. | Miniature craft. | Viet-
nam War, 1961 1975. | War games. | CRAFTS & HOBBIES/
Miniatures | HISTORY/Asia/Southeast Asia | HISTORY/Mili-
tary/General | HISTORY / Wars & Conflicts/Vietnam War
Classification: LCC U311.F37 2022 | DDC 745.59282–dc23

Table of Contents

Rice paddies
(Tim Goodchild)

Introduction

This book is aimed at experienced modelers and wargamers who want to examine the history of the Vietnam War and simulate the actions as tabletop wargames using model figures and vehicles.

The Vietnam War is often depicted as American soldiers patrolling in dense jungles and being ambushed by Viet Cong or PAVN. On the tabletop, this translates to plastic aquarium plants and a handful of infantry on each side. The aim of this book is to encourage more realistic and ambitious games.

Most of the insurgency conflict was fought in agricultural land (e.g., rice paddies and rubber tree plantations) or on wooded hillsides. Important battles were fought on wooded hillsides in the Ashau valley and in the hills near the DMZ. The most desperate fighting took place house to house in the old city of Hue. The Viet Cong were not the significant enemy. Their soldiers were largely dead or captured by February 1968. Only old men and women remained as scouts and informers. The real enemy was the PAVN or NVA. They replaced most of the Viet Cong fighters in South Vietnam by the end 1967 and were the significant enemy from then onward. The NVA committed millions of men to the struggle. Their leaders were communists, but their soldiers were patriots committed to ridding the land of colonial invaders. The war was the largest insurgency war of the cold war period. The US had overwhelming firepower and complete control of the air. However, the North Vietnamese almost always had the initiative.

This is my second book. My first book was *Modelling and Painting World War II German Military Figures*. As the German Army in WWII is popular with people starting the hobby or rejoining as their children grow up, that book was pitched at a beginner level. The Vietnam War is a more niche conflict for wargaming and tends to attract experienced wargamers and modelers. Therefore, this book is about more ambitious projects using a wide variety of techniques.

Michael Farnworth

1.1.1 Acknowledgements

Book Design: Kevin Opp

Illustrator: Tiffany Pettit

Map Illustrators: Julia Lillo and Rocío Espín

Manufacturers and sculptors: Paul Eaglestone, Paul Hicks, and Richard Humble (Empress Miniatures); Simon Osborn (Full Metal Miniatures); Leon Pengilley (Pendraken); Peter Brown (The Assault Group); Edwin Cheung (Rubicon Models), Bob Mackenzie (BobMack3d.com) and Clara Svetoslava Staykova (Barrage Miniatures).

Painters and modelers who provided pictures: Andy Singleton, Ashley Straw, Brad Sanders, John Atter, Mark Hargreaves, Rick Forrest (Danger Close Miniatures), Thomas Riepe, Rubén Torregrosa (heresybrush), John Cuocco, and Gareth Ewart. Also Robert Pye and Thomas McCafferty for help with 3D printing.

Militaria Collections: Geoff Liebrandt and Graham Green

Proofreaders and tutorial testers: Sgt William Hutchinson, Paul Eaglestone and Tommy Le Duc Thinh.

Diorama of "FireBase Pony" central highlands, Vietnam cicra 1968 made by John Cuocco for The American Air Power Museum, Republic Airport, Farmingdale, NY

CHAPTER  1 Introduction to History, Geography and Wargames

1.1 Introduction

This chapter gives historical and geographical background information to the conflict. It also explains some aspects relevant to planning your wargame purchases such as figure scale and wargame type.

1.2 The Opposing Forces

1.2.1 Communists, Viet Minh, & Viet Cong

Western commentators described the Vietnamese as communists. Though true, this is misleading. Very few of the Viet Cong and PAVN soldiers were members of the Communist Party. Most were patriots recruited to defeat and expel foreign invaders. They wanted to end colonialism and unite the country as an independent Vietnamese state.

Indochina had been ruled as a French Colony since 1887. During WWII, the Japanese ruled via a Vichy French government. Ho Chi Minh lead a resistance movement against the Japanese and French in WWII. This was called the Viet Minh (League for the Independence of Vietnam) and was supported by the Americans. At this stage, the Viet Minh was an alliance of many groups. After WWII, the French colonial government was restored and supported by the Americans.

By 1950, the Viet Minh leadership were all communist and were supported with economic and military aid by communist Russia and China. The French were defeated by the Viet Minh in 1954. As a result, the country was split in two, and North Vietnam became an independent communist nation.

The North Vietnamese reorganized the 500,000 Viet Minh fighters into a formal army which became known as the People's Army of North Vietnam. The National Liberation Front NLF of South Vietnam was created by the Viet Minh in 1960 to oppose the South Vietnamese government. The NLF was a political movement with an armed militia, which was called the Viet Cong (Vietnamese communists) by the South Vietnamese and American press.

Strictly speaking, NVA is the North Vietnamese Army and Viet Cong is the militia forces in South Vietnam. PAVN is the People's Army of North Vietnam which means both NVA and Viet Cong. Western journalists often use PAVN and NVA interchangeably.

1.2.2 Free World Forces

Facing the Vietnamese communist forces was an alliance in support of the democratic government. The South Vietnamese forces were called the Army of the Republic of Vietnam or ARVN. The ARVN was supported by the US. In addition, South Korea, Australia, New Zealand, Philippines, and Thailand also sent troops, who were collectively described as the Free World Military Forces. Sometimes the term Free World Forces is used to describe all of these.

1.3 Vietnam— Geography, Climate, & People

The elongated roughly S-shaped country has a north-to-south distance of 1,650 km (1,030 mi) which is equivalent to the distance from Philadelphia to Miami, Florida.

North Vietnam has a temperate climate with four seasons: spring, summer, autumn, and winter. Dien Bien Phu, capital of Dien Bien Province and home of a major battle, is in the mountains in the north where the winter day temperature might be 20°C and drop to 13°C overnight.

The south is tropical with monsoons, so it has two seasons: wet and dry. The southern climate is classed as savannah due to the extensive dry periods. There are very small pockets of tropical rainforest. Saigon has daytime temperatures of 33C to 35C year round and at night it may drop to 21C.

There is very little jungle in Vietnam. Real jungle is less than 5 percent of land mass. Most of the conflict was fought in agricultural land (rice paddies and rubber tree plantations) or on wooded hillsides.

The area south and west of Saigon is the Mekong Delta which is largely agricultural land with rice paddies interspersed with fruit trees and bamboo. Similarly, The Red River Delta, Southeast of Hanoi is a prime agricultural area. The coastline from Nha Trang to Haiphong also has large areas of rice paddies.

There are extensive marshlands in low lying land close to the Cambodian border. North and east of Saigon there are ranges of forested hills which stretch up all the way to the Chinese border. Some parts of the forested areas are sparsely populated. Other parts are occupied by hill tribes and have cultivated areas. There are also some areas of grassland in the central hills.

Ho Chi Minh Trail
In the late 1950s, the Viet Minh supplied their southern forces mostly via junks and fishing boats along the coast. However, this disrupted by the ARVN security forces.

The Ho Chi Minh Trail was established in 1959 to bring men and materials from North Vietnam to the south. The main route was through Laos and started above the demilitarized zone (DMZ) and ended in Cambodia south of Pleiku. There was a second route from Cambodia called the Sihanouk Trail. Together these consisted of hundreds of miles of interconnecting paths and roads. There were multiple interconnecting routes so that damaged sections could be avoided while they were being repaired. Initially these were simple paths and dirt roads, but later many sections were upgraded with asphalt and drainage so that they could operate during the wet season.

Goods were carried on poles or on bicycles, and it took about four months to make the journey. Later, convoys of trucks drove at night between camouflaged staging posts which were 20 to 30 km apart. The drivers, many of whom were women, learned to drive a section of the road at night without lights. At the staging posts, these trucks were unloaded and sometimes loaded with wounded soldiers on their northbound return journey. Southbound goods were put on trucks for the next stage the following night.

The trail was constantly under attack during the day. Two million tons of bombs were dropped on the Ho Chi Minh trail between 1964 and 1973. The trail was protected by anti-aircraft guns, but these could not stop high-level bombing. Thousands of soldiers, engineers, and laborers maintained and repaired the trail. Pipelines and pumping stations were installed, so gasoline and diesel could be delivered to troops in the south without trucks.

Cu Chi
Viet Cong tunnel network to the northwest of Saigon and south of the Iron Triangle.

Iron Triangle
Large area northwest Saigon controlled by Viet Minh in the 1950s and Viet Cong in the 1960s. The area has underground tunnel bases like Cu Chi.

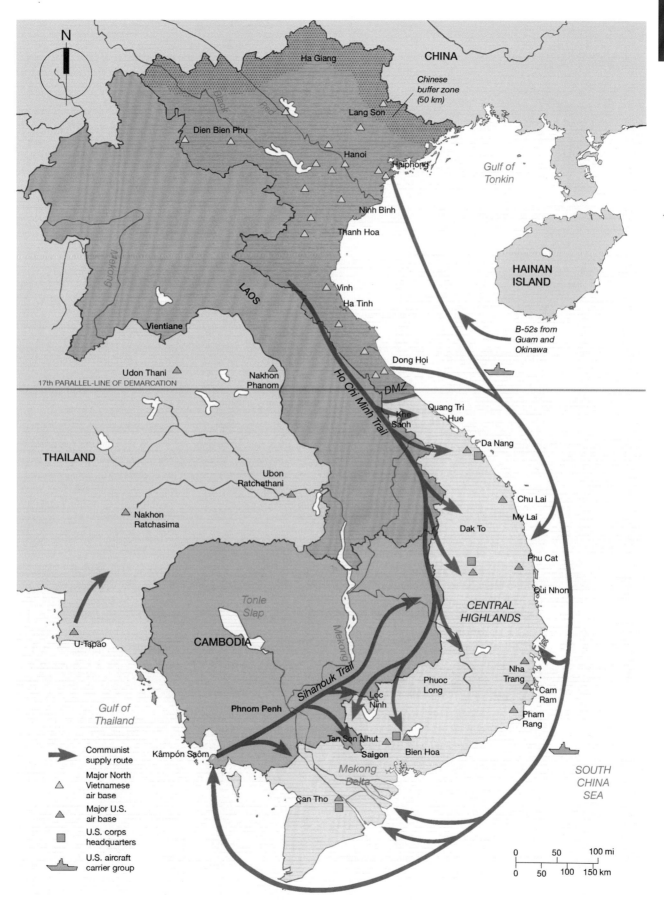

N

Ha Giang
CHINA
Chinese
buffer zone
(50 km)
Lang Son
Dien Bien Phu
Hanoi
Haiphong
Gulf of
Tonkin
Ninh Binh
HAINAN
ISLAND
Thanh Hoa
LAOS
Vinh
Ha Tinh
Vientiane
B-52s from
Guam and
Okinawa
Udon Thani
Nakhon
Phanom
Dong Hoi
17th PARALLEL-LINE OF DEMARCATION
DMZ
Quang Tri
Hue
Khe
Sanh
THAILAND
Da Nang
Ubon
Ratchathani
Chu Lai
My Lai
Nakhon
Ratchasima
Dak To
Phu Cat
Qui Nhon
CENTRAL
HIGHLANDS
Tonle
Sap
CAMBODIA
Nha
Trang
Cam
Ram
U-Tapao
Phuoc
Long
Loc
Ninh
Pham
Rang
Phnom Penh
Gulf of
Thailand
Tan Son Nhut
Saigon
Bien Hoa
Kâmpón Saôm
Mekong
Delta
SOUTH
CHINA
SEA
Can Tho

Ho Chi Minh Trail

Sihanouk Trail

Black
Red
Mekong
Mekong

Communist
supply route

△ Major North
Vietnamese
air base

▲ Major U.S.
air base

■ U.S. corps
headquarters

U.S. aircraft
carrier group

0   50   100 mi
0   50   100 150 km

1.3.2 The Vietnamese People

In 1965, the population of Vietnam was 35 million. The largest ethnic group in Vietnam are the Viet who make up 85 percent of the population.

In 1965, the population was described as being mostly Buddhist, but in reality there were many different folk religions which had elements of Buddhism, Confucianism, and Taoism. Buddhist monks were an important political force in South Vietnam in the 1960s.

About 7 percent of the population are Catholic, though the proportion was higher in 1965. In South Vietnam Catholics were in powerful positions in the government and military. Many Catholics left when the communists took over.

People of Chinese origin are called Hoa and currently make up less than 1 percent of the population. In 1965, there were far more. Chinese owned many commercial and manufacturing companies which were forcibly closed when the communists won in 1975. Approximately 450,000 Chinese left after the war.

Montagnard is a term that was used by the French and Americans to describe the people who lived in the Central Highlands. However, these actually consist of six different ethnic groups. In 1962, the population of the Montagnard people in the Central Highlands was estimated to number as many as one million. The Montagnard peoples were 70 percent Christian and were important allies of the Free World Forces. Many were recruited as soldiers under the Civilian Irregular Defense Group program (CIDG).

In 1968, research on the attitude of the population at Long An 55 km east of Saigon concluded that only 35 percent supported the South Vietnamese government. Twenty percent supported the National Liberation Front (NLF), who were the political arm of the Viet Cong. The remaining 45 percent simply wanted the violence to stop.

1.4
Vietnam War
Timeline

1.4.1 Indochina 1887-1954

After the Napoleonic Wars, the French lost their empire and most of their colonies. Starting in 1830, France established a second French Colonial Empire by conquering large parts of the northwest of Africa, Syria, Madagascar, and Indochina. In 1887, France imposed a colonial government on the countries of Tonkin (North Vietnam), Annam (Central Vietnam), Cochin China (South Vietnam) and Cambodia. Laos was added in 1893. Collectively the countries were called French Indochina. There were many groups of the indigenous people who were opposed to the colonial rulers, and there were several clashes between these groups and colonial forces.

Far away from Indochina, the Russian Revolution was begun in 1917 by the communist Bolsheviks commanded by Vladimir Lenin. The revolution ended rule of the royal Tsars and broke up the Russian Empire. This led to the Russian Civil War fought between communists and anti-communist White Russians. This was won by the Bolsheviks in 1923. The Union of Soviet Socialist Republics (USSR) was established in 1922 under communist rule. After Lenin died in 1924, Josef Stalin took over and ruled until 1953. The USSR actively supported communist groups worldwide.

Between 1923 and 1925, Vietnamese nationalist Ho Chi Minh was trained in the Soviet Union as an agent of the Communist International (Comitern). In1930, Ho Chi Minh founded the Indochinese Communist Party.

WWII started in 1939, and. by June 1940, Nazi Germany had taken control of France. Japan had been at war in China from 1937 and went on to invade French Indochina in 1940. The Japanese allowed the Vichy French to continue ruling Indochina.

In 1941, Ho Chi Minh and communist colleagues establish the League for the Independence of Vietnam. Known as the Viet Minh, the movement aimed to resist French and Japanese occupation of Vietnam. The Viet Minh were given support and encouragement from US OSS. The Viet Minh raided government warehouses and distributed food among the population, thus making them very popular. By the end of WWII, the Viet Minh numbered 500,000.

In August 1945, Japan was defeated by the Allies, ending WWII. The Japanese surrender left a power vacuum in Indochina. In August 1945, the Viet Minh in northern Vietnam took advantage of the Japanese surrender and confiscated their weapons. An estimated 600 Japanese soldiers joined the Viet Minh as leaders and trainers. Ho Chi Minh declared Vietnamese Independence on September 2, 1945. Days later, British-Indian forces landed in the South and the Chinese army crossed into the north to officially accept the surrender of the Japanese to the Allied forces. The Allies had decided to restore French rule. During Operation Masterdom, the British reinstated the Japanese Army under British command to help British-Indian and French troops to fight the Viet Minh rebellion. French troops from Europe began to arrive in early 1946. Operation Masterdom officially finished March 30, 1946, and France took over military control.

After the end of WWII, Russia took over most of Eastern Europe and closed the borders. In 1946, Churchill described this as an Iron Curtain over Eastern Europe. President Harry Truman created the Truman Doctrine, stating that the foreign policy of the United States is to assist any country whose stability is threatened by communism. In 1949, US, Canada, and several West European countries formed NATO. In response, Russia created the Warsaw Pact in 1955. This conflict between communism and its opponents created the Cold War which continued up until 1991.

The Chinese Civil War began in 1927 but paused during the Japanese invasion and occupation from 1937 to 1945. The Chinese Civil War restarted in 1945, and the communists won in 1949. Chinese Communist leader Mao Zedong declared the creation of the People's Republic of China. China went on to support the Korean communists in the 1950 Korean War.

At the end of WWII, Korea was split in two as had been done in Germany. North Korea was under Russian control and South Korea was supported by US and the United Nations. Neither side accepted the division. In 1950, the Korean War started when communist North Korea invaded South Korea, with support from China and Russia. In response, the United Nations, particularly US, British, and British Commonwealth forces supported the South Koreans. After two years of war, each side controlled their original territory. An Armistice Agreement was signed in 1953.

The democratic countries were becoming increasingly worried about communist expansion. In 1954, U.S. President Dwight D. Eisenhower said that the fall of French Indochina to communists could create a "domino" effect in Southeast Asia. This so-called domino theory guided US thinking on Vietnam for the next decade. The dominoes were China, Korea, Vietnam, Laos, Cambodia, Thailand, Malaysia, Indonesia, Burma, and India.

(Wikimedia Commons)

1.4.2 French Indochina War 1946-1954

After WWII, France began to reassert its authority over Vietnam. The French offered limited self-government to Vietnam. Ho Chi Minh rejected this proposal in July 1946, and the Viet Minh began a guerrilla war against the French.

The People's Republic of China and the Soviet Union formally recognized the communist Democratic Republic of Vietnam in January 1950. Both countries begin to supply economic and military aid to communist resistance fighters within the country. Võ Nguyên Giáp, the military commander of the Viet Minh, reorganized his irregular forces to create five full strength infantry divisions. The Viet Minh became a regular army and increased their attacks on French outposts. In response, the US provided military assistance to France.

The scale of battles increased dramatically. Major battles included Cao Băng in 1950 and Hòa Bình in 1951–1952. By 1953, the Viet Minh controlled large parts of the countryside in northern Vietnam and Laos. The French controlled the large towns and cities and had a network on military bases in the countryside. By 1954, French military personnel in Indochina peaked at about 140,000.

Dien Bien Phu
(Wikimedia Commons)

To try to stop the Viet Minh supply routes into Laos, the French sent paratroopers to set up a base in the mountains on the border at Dien Bien Phu. In March 1954, there were 10,800 French troops in the base, as it was besieged by 49,500 Viet Minh. The Viet Minh overran the base on May 7, 1954.

The First Indochina War officially ended on August 1, 1954. This ended French colonial rule in Indochina. The Geneva Accords divided Vietnam at the 17th parallel. The border between North Vietnam and South Vietnam was a Demilitarized Zone, between 7 and 10 km wide and following the line of the Ben Hai River.

In North Vietnam, the communist government followed Stalinist policies. They confiscated land and property from wealthy land owners and the Catholic church. They set up collective farms and nationalized manufacturing industries. Organized religion was discouraged. A million people fled to the south including the wealthy and many Catholics.

1.4.3 US War in Vietnam 1955 -1975

Catholic nationalist Ngo Dinh Diem had been the prime minister of Vietnam in 1954 and became the president of South Vietnam. He was an unpopular leader, as he showed favoritism to Catholics at the expense of other religions, especially Buddhists. Buddhism and similar folk religions made up the vast majority of the population, but the Catholic church was the largest landowner. Catholics also held high positions in the police and the army. Diem survived a bombing of the presidential palace in February 1962.

Ho Chi Minh became President of North Vietnam and served in this role until 1965, though he retained the title until his death in 1969. Võ Nguyên Giáp served as commander-in-chief of the People's Army of Vietnam and deputy prime minister.

North Vietnamese forces began to build a supply route through Laos and Cambodia to South Vietnam in 1959. The route became known as the Ho Chi Minh Trail and was greatly expanded and enhanced during the Vietnam War.

In South Vietnam in 1960, the National Liberation Front (NLF) formed with North Vietnamese backing as the political wing of the anti-government insurgency in South Vietnam. The US viewed the NLF as an arm of North Vietnam and started calling the military wing of the NLF the Viet Cong, short for Vietnam Cong-san or Vietnamese communists. For the next 15 years, the Viet Cong waged an insurgency campaign in South Vietnam.

1962

President John F. Kennedy sent helicopters and M113s as aid to the ARVN in South Vietnam. The US set up the Military Assistance Command, Vietnam (MACV). US Special Forces deployed 400 Green Berets to South Vietnam in May 1961, authorized to perform secret operations against the Viet Cong. They were joined by a small number of SEALs in 1962. Operation Ranch Hand began in 1962 with US aircraft starting to spray Agent Orange and other herbicides over rural areas of South Vietnam to kill vegetation that would offer cover and food for guerrilla forces. US Intelligence now estimated that the Viet Cong controlled 50 percent of the Mekong Delta. In October, the Cuban Missile Crisis gripped world attention, as the US blockaded Cuba to prevent Russia placing nuclear missiles on the island. The Russians backed down and withdrew the missiles.

1963

On January 2, 1,200 ARVN troops, supported by 15 US helicopters, made a three-pronged attack at the village of Ap Bac, in the Mekong Delta. However, the ARVN were ambushed and pinned down by 350 Viet Cong fighters in bunkers and trenches. Thirteen M113 APCs and 300 paratroopers were sent is as reinforcements. The ARVN and US lost 6 dead, 108 wounded, and 5 helicopters. The victorious Viet Cong force suffered 18 killed and 39 wounded. The Viet Cong withdrew silently, in good order during the night.

From May to November, there were widespread protests by Buddhists. Police suppressed the Buddhist Crisis protests with water cannon and tear gas as well as shot several protesters dead. In August, ARVN special forces attacked pagodas and arrested the protestors. Hundreds of Buddhist protesters simply disappeared, killed by the special forces. The US government threatened to withdraw support for South Vietnam. On November 1, ARVN generals staged a coup d'état that was carried out with the tacit support of US officials. President Diem was assassinated by the ARVN in an M113 APC. Between 1963 and 1965, South Vietnam had 12 different governments. In November 1963, President Kennedy was assassinated in Dallas, Texas and Lyndon B. Johnson become president. General William Westmoreland arrived in Vietnam and later became commander of MACV.

1964

On August 5, a North Vietnamese torpedo boat *allegedly* attacked the US destroyers Maddox and Turner Joy in the Gulf of Tonkin. President Johnson submitted the Gulf of Tonkin Resolution to "take all necessary measures to repel any armed attack against the forces of the United States." By this point, there were 23,000 US troops in Vietnam, and roughly 400 had been killed. In South Vietnam, there were 200 Viet Cong insurgency attacks every week. December 28 was the start of the five-day battle of Binh Gia, 50 km east of Saigon, which resulted in 1,800 Viet Cong defeating 4,300 ARVN in the largest battle to date.

1965

Operation Rolling Thunder, the bombing of the North and the Ho Chi Minh Trail began in March 1965 and continued until November 1968. In 1965, the Soviets and Chinese increased military support to North Vietnam. In March, US Marines landed at Da Nang. Operation Starlite deployed 5,500 US Marines in August to attack a Viet Cong regiment 120 km south of Da Nang.

Operation Starlite, 1965
(US Military)

In October, NVA besieged the US base at Plei Me, which was manned by US and ARVN special forces and 400 Montagnard CIDG soldiers. The siege was broken after six days. The NVA employed a new close contact tactic of "grab them by the belt buckle," to avoid being destroyed by the airstrikes and artillery. In November, the first major battle involving US troops occurred at Ia Drang Valley in Central Highlands near Pleiku. Over five days of heavy fighting, approximately 1,000 US Air Cavalry infantry were transported in and out by helicopter. They faced at least 2,500 NVA regulars. Frontline troops on both sides received 50 percent casualties.

1966

In 1966, US troop numbers in Vietnam increased to 385,300. An estimated 75 percent of South Vietnam was under Viet Cong control. During a search and destroy mission on April 11, at Xa Cam My, 134 men of Charlie Company, 2nd Battalion, 16th Infantry Regiment were ambushed by Viet Cong, resulting in 36 dead and 71 wounded.

Australian forces were ambushed in a rubber plantation at Long Tam in August. The Battle of Dak To was fought from November 3 to 23 by US Army and ARVN forces engaged with PAVN near Kon Tum.

President Lyndon B. Johnson with General William Westmoreland (US Military)

1967

Operation Junction City began on February 22 and lasted 82 days. This "hammer and anvil" operation took place north of Saigon. US Armored Cavalry drove the Viet Cong toward strong US army positions. The US deployed 30,000 troops to face an estimated 15,000 in the area. Operation Attleboro was a large-scale search and destroy mission conducted in November against large units of Viet Cong and NVA operating in Binh Doung Province.

By the end of 1967, there were 485,600 US troops in Vietnam. The war was unpopular and there were protests in Washington, D.C., New York City, and San Francisco. These protests continued to increase during the next two years and would later force the government to withdraw US soldiers from Vietnam.

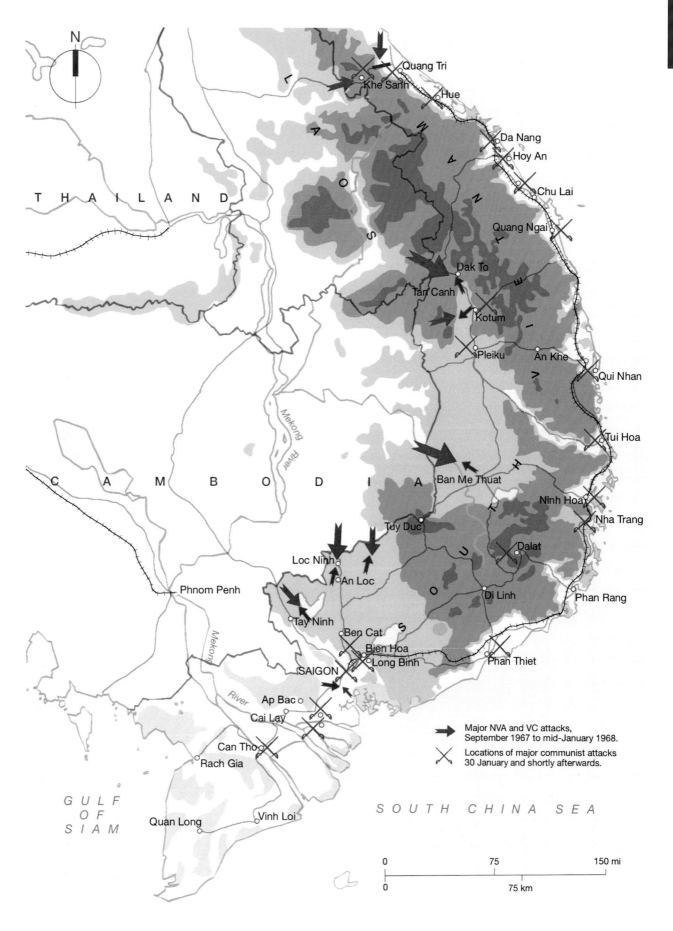

Major NVA and VC attacks,
September 1967 to mid-January 1968.

Locations of major communist attacks
30 January and shortly afterwards.

*101st Airborne soldier during
Operation Cook in 1967.*
(US Military)

1968

1968 began with a siege of the US base at Khe Sanh, which lasted 77 days. On January 30, the Tet Offensive was launched. About 85,000 PAVN and Viet Cong launched hundreds of coordinated attacks on military bases, airfields, towns, and cities throughout South Vietnam. Most of these attacks were quickly repulsed. Fierce fighting in Hue lasted until March 2. On February 6, 14 PAVN PT76 tanks entered South Vietnam via Laos and attacked the Lang Vei Special Forces Camp. On March 16, US troops killed many civilians at Mai Lai. Also in March, President Johnson halted bombing in Vietnam north of the 20th parallel. Richard M. Nixon won the November US presidential election on the campaign promises to restore "law and order" and to end the draft.

1969-1975

On March 3, 1969, PAVN troops with 10 PT-76 tanks attacked Ben Het Camp which was defended by 4 M48A3 Patton tanks. This was the only tank to tank battle between US troops and PAVN. Starting in March 1969 in Operation Menu, B-52 bombers target communist bases in Cambodia. In May 1969, US Airborne and ARVN troops assaulted Ap Bia mountain (Hill 937) for 10 days. Reporters called this brutal battle Hamburger Hill, and it became symbolic of the futility of the Vietnam War. Later that year, President Nixon introduced Vietnamization whereby US troops in Vietnam were reduced from 549,000 in 1969 to 69,000 by 1972.

In February 1970, US National Security Advisor Henry Kissinger began secret peace negotiations with Hanoi politburo member Le Duc Tho in Paris. In April 1970, US and South Vietnamese forces launch the Cambodian Incursion. The last major battle between US troops and PAVN was 23 days of fighting at Fire Support Base Ripcord in July 1970.

During Operation Lam Son 719, ARVN troops with US support invaded Laos in January 1971 in an attempt to cut off the Ho Chi Minh Trail. The PAVN and the ARVN engaged each other with tanks for the first time in February 1971.

French at Dien Bien Phu. Empress Figures (Tim Goodchild)

The 1972 Easter Offensive was an unsuccessful attempted invasion of South Vietnam. 45,000 PAVN with 100 tanks crossed the DMZ and were stopped at a defensive line just north of Hue. A second attack crossed the border at Loc Ninh with 35,000 PAVN and 50 tanks advanced to An Loc where there was fierce fighting. A third attack in the Central Highlands by 40,000 PAVN and Viet Cong took Dak To and were stopped by US airstrikes at Kon Tum in May. By October, most of the lost territory had been retaken. Operation Linebacker was the resumption of bombing of Hanoi and Haiphong.

January 27, 1973, representatives of all sides agreed to end the war at meetings in Paris. US troops were withdrawn on March 29, 1973. North Vietnam returned 591 American prisoners of war in Operation Homecoming.

President Nixon resigned in August 1974 after the Watergate Scandal. In December 1974, 15,000 PAVN attacked the ARVN military bases around Phuoc Long and captured them three weeks later. This gave the PAVN control of the highlands northeast of Saigon. This was the prelude to the Spring Offensive, which ended the war. On March 10, PAVN forces attacked Ban Me Thout. This forced the ARVN to withdraw from Kon Tum and Pieku and retreat to the coast pursued by the PAVN and Viet Cong. By the end of March the PAVN had reached the sea. Simultaneously, PAVN advances forced ARVN to retreat to the coastal cities of Hue, Da Nang, and Chu Lai. 7,000 ARVN were taken prisoner.

By April 3, 1975, the PAVN controlled everything north of Cam Ranh. Surprised by how quickly they had taken central Vietnam, the North Vietnamese decided to move on Saigon immediately. The last phase was called the Ho Chi Minh Campaign. The South Vietnamese tried to block the advance at Xuan Loc and committed one third of their remaining 25,000 ARVN forces to the battle. The ARVN held Xuan Loc for 12 days until April 22. The PAVN encircled Saigon and prepared for the final battle. On April 29, the PAVN attacked Saigon. The Americans began Operation Frequent Wind, the evacuation of 8,000 Americans and South Vietnamese. The following morning, North Vietnamese troops enter downtown Saigon and the South Vietnamese government surrendered unconditionally. In July, North and South Vietnam were formally unified as the Socialist Republic of Vietnam under communist rule.

In 1975, President Gerald R. Ford ruled out any further US military involvement in Vietnam. By the end of the war, more than 58,000 Americans lost their lives. Vietnam would later release estimates that 1.1 million North Vietnamese and Viet Cong fighters were killed, up to 250,000 South Vietnamese soldiers died, and more than 2 million civilians were killed on both sides of the war.

After reunification in 1975, the communist government introduced Stalinist policies. Organized religious practice was discouraged. Former ARVN military and government workers were sent to retraining camps, sometimes for several years. Many businesses were closed down as the state took over. In 1979, there was the Sino-Vietnamese War, a four-week confrontation with China. Hundreds of thousands tried to leave, often by boat. Many Vietnamese boat people were Christians and ethnic Chinese.

1.4.4 Media & Misconceptions

Nineteen
Paul Hardcastle's 1985 single, "Nineteen," was a hit reaching number 1 in many European nations and number 15 in the US Billboard Hot 100. Launched to mark the 10th anniversary of the war, the song was written to highlight the plight of 800,000 veterans suffering with

PTSD following service in Vietnam. The song and video featured samples of narration, newsreel, and interviews set to electro pop dance music. It reached gold status in UK, Canada, and Germany.

The song's lyrics describe that the average age of an infantryman in Vietnam was 19 and was exposed to hostile fire every day of a 12 month tour.

The actual average age of American soldiers killed in Vietnam was 23 not 19. The average age of infantryman was 22. The song is correct that the average man who fought in WWII was 26 years of age. The song is also correct about the intensity of serving in Vietnam. The average infantryman in the South Pacific during World War II saw about 40 days of combat in four years. The average infantryman in Vietnam saw about 240 days of combat in one year thanks to the mobility of the helicopter.

In terms of deaths, 86 percent of the Americans who died in Vietnam were Caucasians, 12.5 percent were black, and 1.2 percent were other races. Two-thirds of the men who served in Vietnam were volunteers, whereas two-thirds of the men who served in WWII were drafted. Approximately 70 percent of Americans killed in Vietnam were volunteers.

1.5
Wargaming the Vietnam War

1.5.1 The Nature of Combat in the Vietnam War

The Vietnam War was very different from WWII. In conventional wars, armies occupy territory, and there is usually a clear front line which divides the forces. In Vietnam, most of the land was not controlled by either side. In many rural areas, up to 25 percent of the population was sympathetic to the Viet Cong cause. As Free World Forces patrolled the rural areas, the Viet Cong went into hiding but reappeared as soon as Allies moved on.

For most of the war, the US and Allies had control of the air and access to massive force, with aircraft, helicopter gunships, tanks, and artillery. The Free World Forces could deploy rapidly using helicopters and APCs. By contrast, the Viet Cong only had light infantry. In South Vietnam, the Viet Cong were well established with secret underground bunkers and stores. The Viet Cong avoided stand up battles, because they were massively outgunned. Instead, they preferred to use infiltration, booby traps, and ambushes. The Americans supplied fuel and food to their bases using convoys of trucks, and these convoys were frequently ambushed. To protect the convoys, armored gun trucks were built by US soldiers.

Most of the NVA actions were infantry without heavy support. The NVA had trucks, tanks, and artillery, but, without air superiority, they were vulnerable. The NVA used extensive artillery to support actions near to the DMZ, such as the siege of Khe Sanh. The NVA had underground bases in the hills of the Central Highlands, and these featured in many battles.

Contrary to popular opinion, very little fighting took place in jungle. There were hundreds of skirmishes among the villages and rice paddies in South Vietnam. The long elephant grass and wooded hillsides of the Central Highlands hosted desperate battles. The Tet Offensive led to a month of house to house fighting in the ancient city of Hue.

There were very few tank battles, and most took place after the US troops left. In February 1968, 14 NVA PT76 light tanks attacked a US base at Lang Vei and 50 percent of them were destroyed. During the Easter Offensive in March 1972, the NVA invaded the south with 322 tanks and AFVs and lost 75 percent of them. In the decisive 1975 Spring Offensive, the NVA invaded the South with 2,000 tanks and AFVs.

Possible Scenarios
- US Army search & destroy mission in paddy fields & villages
- SF monitoring Ho Chi Minh Trail
- Supply truck convoy ambushed by Viet Cong
- US company ambushed by PAVN
- Tunnel Rats – exploring Viet Cong tunnels
- Hill Assault (Central Highlands)
- House to house in Hue

Italeri's Operation Silver Bayonet is 1/72 scale "battle in a box" contains 100 plastic soldiers, a M48 tank, an M113, UH-1 helicopter and two buildings. (Michael Farnworth)

1.5.2 Models for Wargaming the Vietnam War

There are many history books and TV documentaries about the Vietnam War. There are also many iconic feature films, such as The Deer Hunter (1978), Apocalypse Now (1979), Platoon (1986), Full Metal Jacket (1987), and Danger Close (2019).

Vietnam has long been a popular subject for scale models and dioramas. There are numerous kits in 1/35, 1/48 and 1/72 from Tamiya, Academy, Revell, and Master Box. There are some 20 mm (1/72) metal figure ranges such as Platoon 20 that date back to the 1980s. Pendraken started their comprehensive range of Vietnam War figures and vehicles in 12 mm (1/150) in about 2000. The Assault Group launched a comprehensive set of 28 mm (1/56) metal figures in 2003. Corgi produced collectors 1/50 scale vehicles and helicopters in 2000-2010.

Up until 2010, there was clearly some reluctance to wargame Vietnam. This is changing as the main events occurred 50 years ago. It also changed because the war on terror brought modern wargames to computer screens and tabletops. In 2011, Osprey launched Force on Force rules for modern skirmishes. They followed with a scenario book for Vietnam. In 2016, Battlefront launched a rulebook and comprehensive range in 15 mm (1/100).

In 2017, a 10-part American television documentary series, "The Vietnam War," written by Geoffrey C. Ward and directed by Ken Burns was first shown. This is regarded as the definitive history and has brought new focus on the period. Since 2018, Empress Miniatures, Full Metal Miniatures, and Gringos 40s Miniatures have all been investing heavily in new ranges of 28 mm metal figures and resin vehicles. Rubicon Models have announced plans for an extensive range of 28 mm (1/56) scale plastic vehicle and figure kits.

There is a thriving eBay market for 1/50 scale Corgi vehicles and helicopters. There are many supporting scenery products such as MDF building kits from Sarissa Precision and Warbases. Barrage Miniatures offers resin houses and boats in two scales. 3D print on demand services, such as Butler's Printed Models and the tank factory, offer vehicles and scenic items in many scales. In mainstream hobby stores, Italeri launched a 1/72 scale battle in a box set in 2018. Since 2019, there have been three Kickstarter projects offering 3D Printing STL files for vehicles, figures, and buildings from the Vietnam War.

Person height in feet	Person height in inches	Person height in mm	Scale 1/	Figure height foot to top of head in mm	Figure height foot to eye in mm
6 ft	72	1829	35	52	47
6 ft	72	1829	48	38	34
6 ft	72	1829	56	33	30
6 ft	72	1829	72	25	23
6 ft	72	1829	100	18	17
6 ft	72	1829	120	15	14
6 ft	72	1829	150	12	11
6 ft	72	1829	300	6	6

American Soldiers Chart

Person height in feet	Person height in inches	Person height in mm	Scale 1/	Figure height foot to top of head in mm	Figure height foot to eye in mm
5 ft 3 in	63	1600	35	46	47
5 ft 3 in	63	1600	48	33	34
5 ft 3 in	63	1600	56	29	30
5 ft 3 in	63	1600	72	22	23
5 ft 3 in	63	1600	100	16	17
5 ft 3 in	63	1600	120	13	14
5 ft 3 in	63	1600	150	11	11
5 ft 3 in	63	1600	300	5	6

Vietnamese Soldiers Chart

1.5.3 Figure Size & Scale

Model soldiers are made in a variety of sizes. Military and aviation models are sold as scale models, which means that all the dimensions have been scaled down proportionately. For example, an object that is 2 meters tall becomes 20 cm tall at one-tenth scale. Common scales for scale models are 1/16, 1/32 or 1/35, 1/48, and 1/72 or 1/76.

Wargame figures are often sold by size rather than scale; e.g., 28 mm, 20 mm, 15 mm, 10 mm, or 6 mm. To complicate matters further, many wargame figures are measured foot to eye, so a 28 mm figure will actually be 30 mm to the top of the head.

American soldiers were representative of the general population between the ages of 18 and 40. Heights would vary from about 5 feet to 6 feet tall, which translates to 27 mm to 33 mm in 1/56 scale. Vietnamese men averaged 5 foot 3 inches which is 29 mm in 1/56 scale.

Many wargamers are concerned about compatibility of figures, but figure height is a poor indicator. Equipment, however, should always be consistent in size. Therefore, it is best to judge compatibility by comparing figures side by side. Even significant differences can be managed, if figures are kept in separate units so that different sizes and sculpting styles are not adjacent.

Bases

As you plan your army, it is important to select a basing system that will work with your chosen wargames rules.

Individual 28 mm figures on round 25 mm bases are used in many skirmish games. Heavy weapons and artillery are often based as a weapon with crew as miniature dioramas. Some people make the figures removable to simulate casualties while others fix everything down and use casualty markers instead.

20 mm figures are often mounted individually on 20 mm-diameter circles for skirmish games. Sometimes figures are mounted in groups of two to four on rectangular bases to represent a squad or even a platoon.

15 mm, 10 mm, and 6 mm figures are usually mounted in groups of three or four figures on rectangular or square bases. These can represent a squad, a platoon, a company, or even a reg-

Comparison of metal figure sizes 28mm Empress, 20mm Elheim and 12mm Pendraken (Michael Farnworth)

40mm
30mm
20mm
10mm
0mm

iment. According to the definition of the games for larger formations than a platoon, one figure may represents 10 or more men. For wargames involving battalions, a base with a few figures is used to represent a platoon or a company. Divisional and corps wargames are usually played with maps and counters.

1.5.3 Choosing Wargame Rules

Before you choose a set of wargame rules, you will need to decide on the level of warfare that you want to represent. Here are typical military terms based on US Army structures and the number of soldiers that they represent.

- Squad – 4 to 10 soldiers (Staff Sgt.)
- Platoon – 3 to 4 squads: 16 to 40 soldiers (Lieutenant)
- Company or Battery or Troop – 3 to 4 platoons: 100 to 200 soldiers (Captain)
- Battalion – 3 to 5 companies: 500 to 600 soldiers (Lt. Col.)
- Brigade or Regiment – 3 or more Battalions: 3,000 to 5,000 soldiers (Colonel)
- Division – 3 Brigades: 10,000 to 18,000 soldiers (Maj. General)
- Corps – 2 to 5 divisions: 20,000 – 40,000 soldiers (Lt. General)

The US Marine Corps had a different structure up to battalion level based on a triangular concept. Three fire teams to a squad, three squads to a platoon, three platoons to a company with possibly a weapons platoon attached, and three companies to a battalion. The triangular concept gave commanders at all levels top to bottom a good deal of tactical flexibility. Also, down to fire team level, each unit had a trained commander.

List of Vietnam Wargame Rules

Wargames rules can be grouped by the scale of the actions that they represent. Tabletop wargames where one figure represents one man are often referred to as skirmish games. Games for battalion actions above usually have stands of a few figures which represent a platoon in real life.

Squad to platoon (representing up to 40 soldiers per side) 20 mm to 28 mm
- Body Count
- BOHICA
- Bolt Action Vietnam – Viet Cong on the Trail
- Force on Force & Ambush Alley
- Spectre Operations
- Rubicon Vietnam Rules (due 2022)

Platoon to company (representing up to 200 soldiers per side) 15 mm to 28 mm
- DMZ Second Tour (Chain of Command)
- The Long Road South (Disposable Heroes)

Company to battalion (representing up to 1000 soldiers per side) 10 mm to 20 mm
- Charlie Don't Surf
- Rapid Fire Vietnam

Battalion to brigade (representing up to 5,000 soldiers per side) 6 mm to 15 mm
- Cold War Commander (by Pendraken for 1/150 = 12 mm)
- 'Nam 1965-1972 (Battlefront, Flames of War, Team Yankee for 15 mm)

Pendraken 1/150
scale figures are
12mm tall and
suitable for large
games.
(Leon Pengilly)

Descriptions of Vietnam Wargame Rules

Body Count: *Wargames Rules for the Vietnam War.* Written by Ian and Nigel Drury and published by Tabletop Games 2nd Ed 1988. 36 pages. Players are the "Free World" and the Viet Cong/NVA are umpire controlled. Quite a different gaming concept to most others.

BOHICA is a dedicated set of wargame rules for Vietnam from Empress Miniatures that is based on their modern combat rules Danger Close. The name comes from a US military phrase "Bend Over, Here it Comes Again". It is an 80-page full-color softback book which includes rules for infantry, vehicles, and helicopters.

Bolt Action Vietnam: VC on the Trail is a fan generated version of WWII rules, infantry skirmish with possibility to add vehicles, boats, and aircraft. Facebook Group has 2000 members. Update 1.61 published in 2020 (Very Popular)

Charlie Company from RAFM. Published 1997, 76 pages. Platoon-sized forces suitable for campaigns with the aim being to get through a tour of duty.

Charlie Don't Surf by Two Fat Lardies, published 2010, 105 pages as PDF or hard cover. Company level including vehicles, boats, and aircraft. Facebook Group has 600 members. Also a scenario supplement Surf's Up (Very Popular) Charlie Don't Surf are company level and card driven.

DMZ Second Tour is a fan-generated 44-pages PDF supplement for Chain of Command (Two Fat Lardies). DMZ are platoon level and use the same dice activation system as Chain of Command.

Force on Force & Ambush Alley is an infantry skirmish with possibility to add vehicles, boats, and aircraft. FOF is a 224-page rulebook. Ambush Valley is 192-page Vietnam scenario book. AA published 2007, FOF and AV published by Osprey 2011. (PDF Only. Printed is OOP) (Very Popular)

Giặc Mỹ small unit insurgency combat rules created in 1978. Probably the first set of Vietnam specific rules.

Mourir Pour l'Indochine: new set of rules launched in 2022 which cover 1946 to 1954.

'Nam 1965-1972: published by Osprey in 2018, based on Battlefront Team Yankee & Flames of War rules for 15 mm battalion level including vehicles, boats, and aircraft, (Out of Print). Based on FOW supplement Tour of Duty published 2013, 132 pages.

Rapid Fire Vietnam: 2011 fan-generated version of WWII Rules published in 1994. Company level including vehicles, boats, and aircraft.

Rubicon Models are developing a set of Vietnam, called Oscar Mike, which are due to be launched in 2023.

Spectre Operations is a popular ultra-modern wargame designed for a few figures each side.

Comparison of 20mm or 1/72 figures. Left to Right, Elheim USMC, Italeri US Army, Elheim PAVN, Italeri PAVN. (Michael Farnworth)

Comparison of 28mm figures. Left to Right, Empress Viet Minh, Empress VC, Empress PAVN, Rubicon VC, Gringo40s VC, Full Metal Miniatures VC, The Assault Group VC

Comparison of 28mm figures. Left to Right, Empress French, Empress Australian, Empress USMC, Rubicon USMC, Gringo40s USMC, Full Metal Miniatures USMC, The Assault Group Rambo

A member of 2nd Platoon,
Company D, 2nd Battalion,
7th Cavalry, 3rd Brigade,
1st Cavalry Division (Airmo-
bile) carrying an M72 rocket
launcher (Light Anti-Tank
Weapon, LAW) on his back
during Operation Jeb Stuart,
1968. (US Military)

CHAPTER

2 Soldiers

This chapter focuses on the soldiers from North and South Vietnam, America, Australia, and France. It explains their uniforms and equipment. Relevant camouflage patterns are described with notes as to who wore which patterns and when. There are brief notes about insignia and weapons. Figure building techniques are described including soft plastic, white metal, hard plastic kits, and 3D prints. There are painting recipes for wargame figures covering the main combatants, civilians, and water buffalo.

2.1 Techniques for preparing Wargame Figures

2.1.1 Soft Plastic Figures

The cheapest way to wargame the Vietnam War is to use 1/72 scale plastic figures. Italeri makes a boxed set called Vietnam 1965 Battle Box – Operation Silver Bayonet. This big box battle set was launched in 2018. It contains 50 US soldiers, 50 NVA or Viet Cong, an M48 tank, M113 ACAV and a UH-1 Huey helicopter, plus two MDF buildings and a plastic battlefield accessories set. This tutorial uses 1/72 scale figures from the Italeri battle box. These figures were the figures created in 1986 by Esci and have been branded as Revell and Italeri. The US box contains 50 figures in 15 poses, and each US figure is 24 mm tall. The Viet Cong/NVA set also contains 50 figures in 15 poses, and each Vietnamese figure is 23 mm tall.

Clean and Assemble the Figures.
Remove the figures from the sprue with flush cut clippers. Sand the underside of the bases flat by sliding the figure back and forth along an emery board.

One problem with soft polyethylene figures is that they often have flash, and this is difficult to remove. Sanding or filing does not work as it simply makes the surface furry. The best way is to carefully slice the flash away with a scalpel.

Base the Figures.
Mount the infantrymen on 20 mm diameter x 2 mm thick laser cut MDF bases. Alternatively, you can use old coins or steel washers. Fix them in place with cyanoacrylate gel adhesive.

Groundwork with Milliput.
Make a thin sausage of Milliput and blend figure bases into the wargames base so that the contours are smooth

Painting.
It is often said that soft plastic figures cannot be painted. While it is true that paint does not stick very well to polyethylene, this can be overcome with a suitable primer. Acrylic gesso is essentially a mixture of acrylic paint and PVA glue. This will stick to the figure and dry to form a flexible skin, which will take other acrylic paints very well.

2.1.2 Hard Plastic Figures

Before you can start to put any paint on to your hard-plastic miniatures, you need to prepare them. This involves cutting the parts from the sprues, removing mold lines, assembly, and basing.

Cut from sprue. (Michael Farnworth)

Assemble legs to the base. Then add the torso if it is separate.

Dry fit the arms and weapon making sure that they are a matching set before assembling with glue. Add the head and tilt it in an appropriate direction.

Add the pouches and backpack.

For this project, you need a good set of flush or sprue cutters, a sandpaper nail file, a small round file, and a scalpel.

Airfix, Italeri, Perry, Tamiya, and Warlord all make kits using hard polystyrene. The correct glue for hard polystyrene is one containing methyl ethyl ketone (MEK). Revell Contacta Liquid is ideal and is available with an easy-to-use brush applicator.

Rubicon Viet Cong & USMC
Rubicon launched their Viet Cong and USMC figures in 2022. They also will have NVA, ARVN, Australian, and US Army sets. These are plastic multi-pose figures made from tough ABS plastic. The sculpting is very good and each box contains a good range of weapons and equipment which allow you to build a platoon sized force. Most of the figures are seven or eight parts.

The USMC box includes 32 figures who have M16 assault rifle, M60 Mg, M79 grenade launcher, M72 LAW, Remington shotgun, and two that can have a M14 rifle. The Viet Cong box contains 24 men and 8 women, who can be armed with SKS or AK47 rifles, RPG7, and SMGs.

The size is halfway between Gringos 40s and Empress, so the Rubicon figures can be used with either. Height is 28 mm foot to eye, which is about 31 mm to top of the head. Americans and Vietnamese are the same height.

Use Glue for ABS
Rubicon kits are made with ABS which is Acrylonitrile butadiene styrene. This is much harder and tougher than polystyrene. Use a glue that is recommended for ABS, such as Tamiya ABS

Cement or Plastic Magic. Both come in a glass bottle with an easy-to-use brush applicator. Revell Contacta Liquid will work but the finished joints are weak.

Removing Parts from the Sprue

Many people have difficulty cutting parts from the sprue. This is usually because they are using the wrong type of tool. The best way is to use a pair of sprue cutters or a pair of electronics flush cutting pliers. The flat side of the cutter should be pressed close to the part so that there is no long stub. If you do this carefully, there is very little that needs to be sanded away. If the part has a curved section, make additional cuts to remove the stump from the sprue. If you have difficulties, try cutting from the opposite side of the sprue.

The instruction sheet is very useful to help you decide which sets of arms go together and which bodies they fit to. On the USMC sprue, many of the arms are marked with a letter in the shoulder joint, so it is easy to match up right and left sets.

Batches

It is possible to assemble four or more figures at a time. However, the parts are designed as sets, so it is best to have each figure on a separate tray. Cut out one figure at a time and put all the required parts in one tray. Do the same with the next figure in the second tray. As you assemble the figures, glue one or two parts, then place the figure on the tray and leave it to dry. Do the same operation on the next figure.

Tamiya ABS Cement comes in a bottle with a brush applicator, which is usually best for assembling plastic figures. After dry-fitting the parts, paint the glue on the surface to be joined. The active ingredient softens the plastic. Join the parts and hold in place for about 10 seconds. Normally, you only need to coat one side of the joint with glue. However, when attaching arms to bodies, you will sometimes get a better result by coating both sides. When both sides of the plastic joint are soft from the glue, it will naturally fill in any small gaps and make a neat joint.

Assembly Sequence

The easiest assembly sequence is legs, torso, base, arms, head, and then the rest. If the legs are separate from the torso, assemble them first. Once the legs are attached to the body, it is usually advisable to glue them to a plastic base. This could be the final gaming base or simply a temporary base for the build. Arms are usually in pairs and should be tried as a dry fit before gluing, because some sets work on every single body and others look strange. The head comes next, and this usually faces either in the direction that the weapon is pointing or the direction of movement. If the hat is separate, note the egg shape on the underside of the hat, and that the narrow end is the front. Finally, add the appropriate ammunition pouches, canteen, bags, and backpack.

2.1.3 3D Print Figures

Wargames figures can be printed with a 3D resin printer using flexible "tough" resins. Fused Deposition Modelling (FDM) 3D printers are not suitable for small scale figures. The general method for 3D printing using a resin printer is described in the Vehicles chapter.

Where to Buy STL Files

Currently there are very few figures available as STL files. Germania Figuren has an extensive range which are designed for 1/72 (24 mm). Unfortunately, the STL files cost as much as metal figures. Also. the Germania Figuren figures are anatomically sculpted and thus do not match with metal wargames figures.

https://germania-figuren.eu/3D-printer/the-cold-war/Vietnam-War-491/

Figures set up for a resin 3D print. Note that they are leaning backwards so the supports are on the back. (Michael Farnworth)

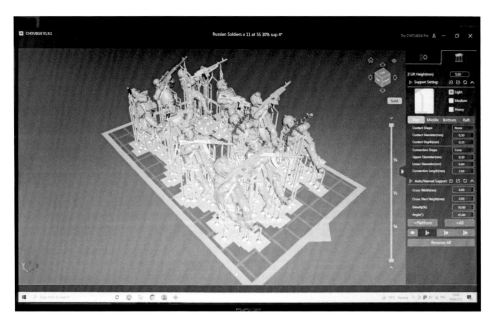

Scale

STL files are usually designed for a particular scale but you can usually scale them up or down. A figure that is designed for 1/72 (24 mm) can be scaled up to 1/56 (28 mm) or even 1/35 (54 mm) without causing printing problems, but it will tend to look chunky and lacking detailed larger scales. Similarly, the same figure designed at 1/72 (24 mm) can be scaled down to 1/144 (12 mm) but some parts will be thin and easily breakable.

Preparation of the STL Files

Once you have bought STL files, you need to prepare them for printing. Load the files into print preparation software such as Chitubox, With the figure standing vertical adjust the height of the figure. Note that a nominally 28 mm figure will be about 32 mm from floor to the top of the helmet. Tilt the figure in the software to 45 degrees with the face and chest uppermost to ensure that the supports are at the back of the figure. Try to use light supports as this will mean there are less marks to clean up on the finished model.

Printing

Figures are best printed with a resin 3D printer using a tough resin. After printing, wash the figure in a suitable solvent such as 99 percent isopropyl alcohol. Then wash again in warm water. While the figures are in the warm water remove the supports. They should break away easily without leaving a noticeable scar. Dry the figures and cure them in ultraviolet light.

Painting

You can paint 3D prints in the same way as a plastic or metal model. Undercoat with either acrylic spray paint or a brush on primer such as acrylic Gesso

2.1.4 Metal Figures

There are several manufacturers of 28 mm white metal figures for Vietnam including Empress, Full Metal Miniatures, Gringos 40s, and The Assault Group. Elheim make 20 mm metal figures for the Vietnam War.

Clean and Assemble the Figures.

Most metal figures come as one-piece castings. The figures should need little cleaning. Check for small silver hairs from mold vents and stubs from the casting sprue. Remove these with flush cut clippers. Sand the underside of the bases flat by sliding the figure back and forth along an emery board.

Sand the base flat by holding the figure and pushing it across a sanding stick. Trim off any threads from the mould vents. (Michael Farnworth)

Attach the figure to a wargame base and blend in the figure base using Milliput.

This machine gun is held in Blutack while the cyanocrylate glue sets.

The base is carefully worked out so that the figures and gun are positioned within the base.

Base the Figures.

Mount the infantrymen on 25 mm diameter x 2 mm thick laser cut MDF bases from Warbases. Alternatively, you can use old coins or steel washers. Fix them in place with cyanoacrylate gel adhesive.

Base the sniper team on a 50 mm diameter x 2 mm thick laser cut MDF base from Warbases. However, to make the figures removable, mount them on 16 mm diameter steel washers and attached to a scenic base with rare earth magnets. The magnets are neodymium disc magnets 10 mm diameter x 0.5 mm thick magnet and are available from Spider Magnets via Ebay.

Groundwork with Milliput.

Note, if you have already decided how to base the figures, it is a good idea to do the groundwork with Milliput before priming the figure. Make a thin sausage of Milliput and blend figure bases into the wargames base so that the contours are smooth.
Using Milliput, the figure bases are blended into the wargames base so that the contours are smooth.

In the case of the sniper team, a small hillock is made. Then parts are pressed flat as a foundation for low walls.

Special care is taken with the sniper team to get the holes at the same depth as the washers, so that there would be no step. To do this, two washers are used as blanks. The washers are wiggled to create a hole very slightly larger than the washers.

Milliput is applied to the base but the figures and machine gun are not attached to the base.

The figures are mounted on corks for painting.

These vehicle crew figures are mounted on a piece of wood for painting.

Figures mounted on 20mm steel washers and MDF base has magnets.

2.1.5 Painting Sequence for Figures

Priming & Undercoating

Batch Sizes

The painting stages from 1 to 4 can be done with a large batch of figures. With practice, it is quite easy to undercoat and prepare 30 figures and these can also be from different armies and periods. The detailed painting of uniforms and equipment is easier in a small batch of say 10 similar figures. Once the painting is completed, the landscaping of the base with sand, grass tufts, etc. can also be done as a large batch of 30 figures. These techniques are the same for metal and plastic figures.

Color	Color	Vallejo Model Color	Item
	Black	Black Acrylic Gesso	Undercoat
	White	White 70.951	Drybrush to bring out details
	Beige Brown	Beige Brown 70.875	Base
	Flesh	Main: Cork Brown 70.843 Shade: Flesh Wash Highlight: Flat Flesh 70.955	Face & Hands (Caucasian and Korean)
	Beige Brown	Main: Beige Brown 70.875 Shade: Flesh Wash	Face and Hands (Vietnamese, Cambodian, Laotian and Thai). Base
	Beige Brown	Main: Beige Brown 70.875 Shade: Dark Brown Wash	Face and Hands (African American, Africans). Base

Step by Step

1. **Prime in Black.** Prime the figures with black acrylic Gesso applied with a brush. Dilute the Gesso with a small amount of water to ensure that it goes on thinly. If you add to much, the paint will tend to draw back and leave gaps.

2. **Overbrush with White.** Overbrush the figures with white. Overbrushing is like dry brushing but with the brush damp with paint, so that it leaves a light coat on the higher areas but does not touch the recesses. This helps with the visualization and makes the subsequent painting steps easier. It gives a brighter base coat which means brighter highlights later. This step also highlights faults such as mismatch or flash. If casting faults are found, trim off vents and file any mismatch smooth.

3. **Paint Exposed Flesh**. Paint the exposed flesh of the hands and feet with a base coat with Cork Brown 70.843 for the Caucasians and Beige Brown 70.875 for the African Americans. Allow this to overlap onto the weapon and the shirt collar. Then, coat the flesh with a wash of Citadel Reikland Fleshshade This dries to emphasize the borders of the face and hands, making it easier to see where the connections are.

4. **Paint the Base**. Paint the bases Beige Brown 70.875.

Undercoat the figure in black.

Drybrush the figure with white to bring out the detail.

Paint the exposed skin and apply a brown wash to bring out detail. Paint the base brown.

Preparation completed.

Paint the uniform with US Dark Green.

Highlight the uniform with 50:50 Dark Green and Stone Grey.

Paint the flak jacket.

Paint the Helmet cover.

*28mm USMC by Gringo 40s
(Michael Farnworth)*

Typical Painting Sequence

1. **Paint the Uniform Dark Green.** Paint the base coat of the uniform. Vallejo Model Color US Dark Green 70.893 is suitable. German Uniform 70.920 can be used as an alternative for new clean uniforms.

2. **Shade the Clothing.** Add highlights with Green Grey 70.886, leaving much of the US Dark Green visible in the recesses. Alternatively, mix 50 percent base color and 50 percent Stone Grey 70.884 to get the highlight shade. A more subtle shading can be achieved by wet blending the stone grey into the dark green directly on the figure.

3. **Paint Helmet Cover Green Grey.** Give the helmet cover a base color of Green Grey 70.886, or the 50:50 mix from the previous step.

4. **Paint the Black Parts.** Paint the rifle, binoculars, and boots with a very dark grey color, e.g., German Dark Grey 70.995. True black will be added later using a wash. Note that the sniper rifle has a black barrel and sight but a wooden stock.

    If you wish to emphasize the metal parts, mix some metallic silver with the dark grey and paint highlights on the weapons.

5. **Paint the Dark Brown Parts.** Using the using German Camo Medium Brown 70.826, paint the wooden parts of the sniper rifle and the Thompson SMG.

6. **Paint the Flak Jacket.** Paint the flak jacket with Khaki Grey 70.880.

7. **Paint the Helmet Cover.** The USMC were issued camouflage helmet covers which were reversible. One side had a brown dappled pattern, and the other side was printed with the Mitchell pattern of green leaves and a few brown twigs.

    Using a small brush, paint twigs as Y shapes using German Camo Medium Brown 70.826. Build up the leaves with dots of Luftwaffe Green 70.823 and German Camo Bright Green 70.833. Later, this was all dulled down with an olive-green wash.

8. **Paint the Eyes (optional).** Paint the eyes with a white horizontal dash and a black dot. This will give oversized and slightly misshapen eyes. Then form correct eye shapes by painting the flesh color above and below. It should be noted that the eyes are only visible if you pick up the figure, so this step is not needed.

9. **Shading with Washes.** Apply washes to emphasize the shading. Citadel Shade colors from Games Workshop are good but need a little practice. Sometimes wash effects

can be quite heavy, so in each case, do an experiment first and, if needed, dilute the shade with water or acrylic Matt Medium to ensure that the shading is subtle enough.

- Give Caucasian flesh a wash of Reikland Fleshshade.
- Wooden parts are washed with dark brown, Agrax Earthshade.
- Give the uniform greens a wash of Athonian Camoshade, or if you prefer a blue green tint, use Coelia Greenshade.
- Shade black parts with Nuln Oil.

2.1.6 Forty Shades of Olive Green

The Americans, Australians, South Koreans, and South Vietnamese all had similar colored uniforms in olive green. US Army and USMC uniforms were made from the same cloth. This looks like a blue green shade of olive green when it is new. For soldiers in the field, dirt and perspiration changed the shades. Over time the sunlight and wear and tear caused the color to fade towards a paler grey tone.

The jackets and trousers are painted with Vallejo Model Color paints with Citadel shade washes.

1. Luftwaffe Camouflage Green 70.823 with wash of Coelia Greenshade.
2. Luftwaffe Camouflage Green 70.823 with wash of Athonian Camoshade.
3. US Dark Green 70.893 with wash of Coelia Greenshade.
4. US Dark Green 70.893 with wash of mixture 50:50 Coelia Greenshade & Athonian Camoshade.
5. German Uniform 70.920 with wash of Athonian Camoshade.
6. German Uniform 70.920 with wash of Coelia Greenshade.
7. German Uniform 70.920 with wash of mixture 50:50 Coelia Greenshade & Athonian Camoshade.

All of the figures were treated with a wash emphasize the shading. This wash is ink mixed with Matt Medium, so that it darkens the recesses in the figure. Citadel Shade colors from Games Workshop are good but need a little practice. Sometimes their wash effects can be quite heavy, so, in each case, do an experiment first and, if needed, dilute the shade with water or acrylic Matt Medium to ensure that the shading is subtle enough. These uniforms are given a wash of Athonian Camoshade. If you prefer a blue green tint, use Coelia Greenshade.

*Dirt, Dead Leaves, Grass,
Jungle Plants, Rubble*
(Michael Farnworth)

2.1.7 Basing for Vietnam

Just Dirt

The earth in Vietnam is reddish brown. Vallejo Beige Brown 70.875 is a useful approximation to the color. The dirt is lighter when it is dry and darker when it is wet. Many paths, military bases, and roads were simply dirt. The wooded areas were also dirt in the dry season.

Put some sand in a plastic bowl. Cover the upper surface of the bases with PVA glue and then dip in the bowl of sand. After sand has been added to all the figures, dilute the remaining PVA glue was with water and color it with a brown color such as German Camo Medium Brown 70.826. Leave this to dry overnight. The following day, highlight the sand with a light drybrush of Iraqi Sand 70.819.

*Sniper and spotter
are removable*

Grass Tufts

In the woodland areas, the ground is strewn with dried leaves and has some grassy tufts. Between the woodlands there are grassy areas. Also, the rural farming areas have grass at the sides of paths and in fields. Follow the steps above and then add a few leaves or grassy tufts. You can also use static grass to simulate larger areas of grass.

Bricks & Rubble

To give an impression of urban rubble, build low walls with individual plaster bricks and PVA glue. The bricks are called Red Bricks (Small) from Pegasus Hobbies.

2.2
Free World Uniforms & Equipment

2.2.1 US Army & USMC Uniforms

Uniforms for both the US Army and USMC were made from the same patterns and identical fabrics. The uniform started off as a blue green shade and faded over time to a much paler grey green.

The first American soldiers in Vietnam wore the OG-107 Cotton Sateen Utility Uniform, commonly described as "utilities." The utility uniform was comprised of a shirt which tucked into trousers. The shirt had vertical pockets and exposed buttons. The pants were a straight leg pant with two patch pockets in the front and two patch pockets with a button flap on the back.

Jungle fatigues were introduced in about 1966 and were authorized for all combat soldiers in 1967. These were comprised of a shirt which had angled pockets and covered buttons. This was not tucked in. Jungle fatigues were produced in cotton poplin up to early 1969. Ripstop cotton was introduced in 1967 but due to low stocks, it was not commonly worn until 1969. Engineer Research & Development Laboratories (ERDL) camouflage jungle fatigues were issued to "elite" troops including SOG, SF, LRRP/Ranger Companies, Force Recon, Navy SEALs, Pathfinders, etc. after 1967. By the end of 1969, UMSC combat units wore ERDL.

US Army early war Utility Uniform, of the 25th Infantry Division who deployed to Vietnam in 1965 and 1966 with full color insignia. (Geoff Liebrandt)

Insignia

US Army soldiers had their surname in capital letters above the right chest pocket. This was initially black lettering on white tape but from summer 1966 this changed to olive green tape. US ARMY in capitalized black letters on olive tape was sewn above the left chest pocket. Tapes were horizontal until September 1969, after which they were slanted parallel to the top of the chest pocket. USMC followed the same system but with US MARINES above the left chest pocket.

Divisional patches were worn on the sleeve at the shoulder. These were full color and usually followed WWII designs until June 1966 when subdued black insignia on olive green were introduced. Units such as the 82nd Airborne Division, 101st Airborne Division, and 1st Infantry Division retained full color insignia throughout the conflict.

Rank insignia also changed to subdued colors beginning in June 1966. Sergeant stripes were worn on both sleeves. Pin-on insignia were introduced from July 1968, so that the soldier could switch it to a clean uniform and make laundry management easier. By 1970, pin-on insignia were normal.

Early war US utility shirt of a Staff Sergeant of 5th Special Forces Group and green beret. In the early part of the war American special forces soldiers went into combat operations in these uniforms with full color patches.
(Geoff Liebrandt)

Jungle Shirt circa 1966 of Staff Sergeant from the 198th Light Infantry Brigade, with subdued insignia.
(Geoff Liebrandt)

Armored crewman helmet
(Geoff Liebrandt)

Black Leather Combat Boots
(Geoff Liebrandt)

3rd Pattern Jungle Boots
(Geoff Liebrandt)

Flak Jackets

Flak Jackets (i.e., bulletproof vests) were made of nylon and featured a more yellowish green color. There were many different types.

Helmets

The steel helmet was very similar to the WWII version. Both the Army and USMC were issued camouflage helmet covers which were reversible. One side had a brown dappled pattern and the other side was printed with the Mitchell pattern of green leaves and a few brown twigs. It was very common for soldiers and marines to write slogans, peace signs, their hometown, "born to be bad," crosses, etc. on the camo cover of their helmets.

Most of the helmets were also supplied with an olive-green webbing band to allow foliage to be added. Soldiers and Marines invariably stuffed items under the helmet band around the camouflage such as cigarettes, a grenade pin, bug repellent, a spoon, etc.

In camp and also on jungle patrols, it was common to wear a soft hat made from the same material as the uniform. The army had "boonie" hats with a wide brim all round. The USMC had a cover, which was a round hat with a bill over the eyes. Marines also wore "boonie" hats from about 1967 onwards. Many soldiers and marines had the brims cut down by Vietnamese civilians. They were then called "Stingy-Brims".

Boots

Black Leather Combat Boots were worn by the US Army until at least 1966 and longer by the USMC. Some sources say that USMC wore all black leather boots in 1968. The M1962 version, commonly called McNamara's had a smooth sole. The 1967 version had a vulcanized rubber ripple sole.

US Army Jungle boots were a combination of black and olive green. The sole, heel cup, forefoot and lace strips are all black leather, but the sides are olive green nylon. Protype Jungle Boots were developed as early as 1962, but were not common until 1966. The upper portion was made of water resistant material that dried quickly when wet. Drain holes were inserted in the lower portion of the boots so that after submersion water that got into the boots had a means of draining out quickly. The first pattern had vulcanized rubber Vibram soles. By the 1966, the 3rd Pattern had a vulcanized rubber Panama sole reinforced with internal plates to protect the wearer from sharpened stakes and other booby traps.

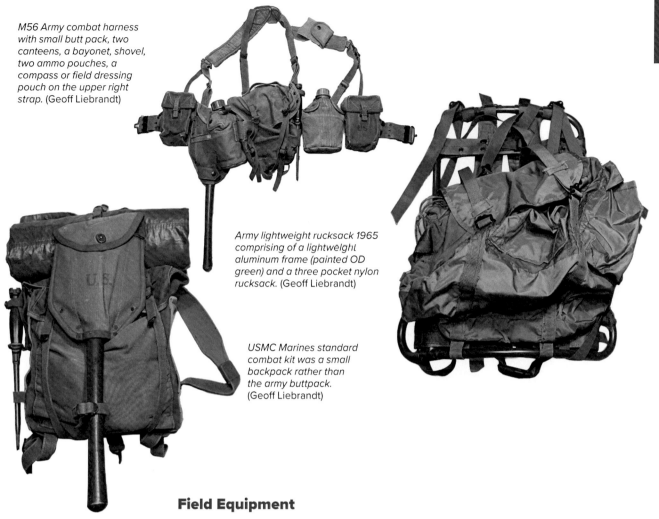

M56 Army combat harness with small butt pack, two canteens, a bayonet, shovel, two ammo pouches, a compass or field dressing pouch on the upper right strap. (Geoff Liebrandt)

Army lightweight rucksack 1965 comprising of a lightweight aluminum frame (painted OD green) and a three pocket nylon rucksack. (Geoff Liebrandt)

USMC Marines standard combat kit was a small backpack rather than the army buttpack. (Geoff Liebrandt)

Field Equipment

Weapons

The M14 Battle Rifle became the standard issue for US Army by 1958 and USMC by 1965. The predecessor was the WWII M1 Garand rifle. The M14 was selective fire and had a 20-round magazine with 7.62 x 51 mm NATO mm cartridges. Most American units in Vietnam changed over to M16 in 1967, but some retained the M14.

Genuine Vietnam era M16 A1 assault rifle, including magazines, bullets, ammo pouches and bayonet. Note the variety of colors for the magazines, the operation manual, gun oil bottle and polythene bag for river crossings. Telescopic sights were not standard with M16. (Graham Green Collection)

US Marine in typical outfit from the 1965 to 1967 period wearing jungle uniform, flak jacket, Mitchell helmet cover, black boots and carrying a M14 battle rifle. Note—the towel round his neck would have been a similar olive green to the uniform. (US Military)

Some US special forces continued using the M1 carbine instead of the M14. The M1 was a selective fire short rifle introduced in 1942 that used a .30 carbine cartridge. It was very light at 6 lbs and only 36 inches (900 mm) long. This weapon was very popular with South Vietnamese forces. During the Vietnam War, 15-round magazines were common, but 30-round banana magazines were also available.

The M16 assault rifle was about two-thirds the weight of an M14 and fired the lighter 5.56×45 mm NATO cartridges. During the Vietnam War M16s were supplied with 20-round magazines. The M16 was made of steel and plastic with no wooden parts. The stock, pistol grip, and front grip were black plastic. Other parts were blackened steel, to a shade called Colt Grey, which is noticeably lighter than the black plastic.

Approximately 1,000 Armalite AR15 were issued to US Special Forces in Vietnam in 1962. The army production version XM16E1 was issued to soldiers in Vietnam in March 1965. This rifle had serious problems that caused it to jam if it was not cleaned regularly. These failures resulted in many deaths in combat. An improved version M16A1 was issued to the US Army from 1967 onward. Some USMC troops adopted the M16A1, but a few retained the older M14. Up until 1968, the M1 carbine was the most common weapon. M1 Garand, M1918 BAR, and M3 Grease Gun were also used. By Tet in January 1968, the ARVN elite units had M16A1 but the Ruff Puffs did not get them until end 1968.

2.2.2 ARVN Uniforms

South Vietnamese forces were equipped with US helmets, weapons, and vehicles. Uniforms were similar in concept to US uniforms but made in Vietnam with locally produced cloth. These were much more slimline in cut than US uniforms, reflecting local fashions. Many soldiers and officers arranged for tailors to make the shirts short sleeved.

Shirt of ARVN 23rd Division sergeant (Geoff Liebrandt)

Shirt of ARVN Ranger Battalion (Geoff Liebrandt)

Insignia

ARVN soldiers had their surname above the right chest pocket with gold lettering on olive green tape. This changed to black lettering if other insignia was subdued. Divisional patches were worn on the sleeve at the left shoulder. Subdued designs were issued by many units but Paratroopers and Rangers and other elite troops retained full color patches. Sergeant stripes were worn on the left sleeve.

Shirt belonging to a Colonel of ARVN 9th Division with paratroop and Ranger qualification patches and metal rank insignia. (Geoff Liebrandt)

Shirt of ARVN 3rd Infantry Division with subdued insignia. (Geoff Liebrandt)

A selection of original ARVN caps. Top left - a cloth billed cap worn by ARVN Rangers and Airborne troopers, as well as VNMC marines. The hat is patterned after the USMC fatigue cap first worn in WW2 and still worn in Vietnam. Top right - another billed cap with ARVN colonel's rank insignia pinned to the front. Bottom left - the red beret of an ARVN Ranger. Bottom right - the dark green beret of a VNMC marine (Geoff Liebrandt)

ARVN Ranger Lieutenant's Biet Dong Quan camouflage shirt with colored insignia. (Geoff Liebrandt)

ARVN "BATA" combat boots. (Geoff Liebrandt)

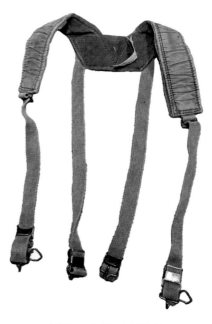

US Army lightweight field harness used by ARVN. (Geoff Liebrandt)

ARVN two pocket backpack. (Geoff Liebrandt)

Quân Lực Việt Nam Cộng Hòa
Army of the Republic of Vietnam

Khỏng Quân Việt Nam
Vietnamese Air Force

Hải Quân Việt Nam
Vietnamese Navy

Vũng 1
Military Region 1

Vũng 2
Military Region 2

Bộ Tổng Tham Mưu QLVNCH
ARVN Joint Chiefs of Staff

Thiết Giáp
Armor Unit

All ARVN armored units used the same general design, with a white number in the blue circle to designate the unit's number

Vũng 3
Military Region 3

Vũng 4
Military Region 4

Pháo Binh
Artillery Unit

All ARVN artillery units used the same general design, with a red number in the white circle to designate the unit's number

Địa Phương Quân/
Nghĩa Quân
Regional Forces/
Popular Forces

Sư Đoàn 1
1st Division

Sư Đoàn 3
3rd Division

2nd pattern
3rd Division insignia
(subdued)

Sư Đoàn 2
2nd Division

The 3rd Division was formed in October, 1971

Sư Đoàn 22
22nd Division

Most ARVN divisions had three regiments. The 22nd Division had four - the 40th, 41st, 42nd, and 43rd Regiments. The extra regiment was needed to cover the large territory assigned to the 22nd Division. Many of the men in this division were hardcases transferred from other units.
(From Phuong V. Nguyen, an officer in this division)

Sư Đoàn 23
23nd Division

Sư Đoàn 5
5th Division

Sư Đoàn 18
18th Division

The 18th Division was formed in 1966 or early 1967. It was briefly numbered the "10th Division" before receiving its final designation.

Biệt Khu Thủ Đô
Capital Military District

Huế

Đà Nẵng

Chu Lai

Phù Mỹ

Ban Mê Thuột

Lai Khê

Xuân Lộc

Củ Chi

Thủ Đô
Sài Gòn

Đồng Tâm

Sạ Đéc

Bạc Liêu

Sư Đoàn 21
21st Division

Sư Đoàn 9
9th Division

Sư Đoàn 7
7th Division

Sư Đoàn 25
25th Division

Biệt Động Quân
Vietnamese Army Rangers

Thủy Quân Lục Chiến
Việt Nam
Vietnamese Marine Corps

Lục Lượng Đặc Biệt
Special Forces

Liên Đoàn 81
Biệt Cách Nhảy Dù
81st Airborne Ranger Group

Sư Đoàn Nhảy Dù
Airborne Division

The Vietnamese Ranger and Marine battalions, Special Forces, the 81st Airborne Ranger Group, and Airborne Division served as the armed forces general reserve. Their headquarters were in Saigon, but they fought wherever they were needed. These units were considered the elite - the toughest and best soldiers of the Republic of Vietnam.

Vinh Danh các chiến sĩ VNCH đã và đang anh dũng chiến đấu cho tự do và dân chủ tại Việt Nam
In tribute to the soldiers of the Republic of Vietnam who fought for freedom and democracy in Vietnam

2.2.3 Australian Uniforms

Australians wore British style jungle green Aertex uniforms. Soldiers are usually wearing bush hats rather than helmets. During the conflict, SAS also used Tiger Stripe camouflage from about 1965 and ERDL green camouflage from about 1968.

Insignia

Australian and New Zealand soldiers tended to wear no insignia in combat zones. Sometimes cords would be threaded through the hat band, but this was more personalization than a rank symbol.

The Australians would wear insignia on base or outside the base, a Brassard (a piece of cloth the wrapped the upper arm) on the left shoulder, the Australian rising sun badge (yellow) under could be the rank for NCOs. These followed the British system of single stripe for lance corporal, twin stripes for corporal, sergeant three stripes, staff sergeant three stripes and crown above, warrant officer crown. Officers wore slide on rank insignia (slide onto the epaulettes) on both shoulders, Sub Lieutenant one pip, Lieutenant two, Captain three, Major wore one crown, Lieutenant Colonel one pip and one crown, and Colonel two pips and a crown.

Weapons

Early in the conflict, the main weapon was the L1 A1 SLR, Self-Loading Rifle also known as the FN FAL rifle. During the Vietnam War, this had a wooden stock and foregrip. Some soldiers used the Owen submachine gun. From 1967, M16 rifles were adopted.

UH-1 Huey spraying defoliant.
(US Military)

Sergeant Curtis E. Hester firing his M-16 rifle, Sergeant Billy H. Faulks calls for air support, Co D, 151st (Ranger) Inf., Vietnam War, 1969. Note that Curtis wears ERDL camouflage in the sand base colorway and Faulks wears Tiger Stripe camouflage in the colors that reenactors describe as silver tiger. (US Military)

2.3 Free World Camouflage Patterns in Vietnam

US forces and their allies used four camouflage patterns during the Vietnam conflict Frog Skin, Tiger Stripe, Mitchell, and ERDL.

Frog Skin pattern was adopted by the USMC in 1942 and used extensively in the Pacific campaign. This pattern is also popular with hunters and is commonly known as Duck Hunter pattern. After WWII, it was supplied to the French and Koreans. During the Vietnam War, some Korean soldiers used this pattern. Montagnard soldiers and some ARVN special forces used a similar pattern called Bao Gam.

During the French Indochina conflict from 1945 to 1955, French paratroopers and the Foreign Legion were issued with both US Frog Skin pattern and French Lizard pattern uniforms. It was quite common to see soldiers wearing Lizard pattern jackets and Frog Skin pattern trousers and vice versa. In the 1950s, South Vietnamese Rangers and Special Forces also adopted French Lizard pattern camouflage.

Tiger Stripe was developed in Vietnam and adopted by the South Vietnamese forces just after the end of the French Indochina War. When the US sent USMAAG military advisors, they adopted Tiger Stripe to match the units with whom they were stationed. Later the pattern was also adopted by many of the US elite forces.

In 1968, US forces started to be issued the ERDL pattern which was the first official US Armed Forces woodland pattern. This was used in parallel with Tiger Stripe by US forces and was adopted by South Vietnamese elite forces.

The Mitchell pattern helmet cover became a very recognizable symbol of the Vietnam War. The helmet covers were worn by US Army and USMC, AVRN, Korean, and Thai soldiers. With the onset of the Vietnam War, most US and Allied soldiers were issued camouflage helmet covers which were reversible. One side had a brown dappled pattern which is often called cloud camouflage, and the other side was printed with the Vine Leaf pattern of green leaves and a few brown twigs.

2.3.1 US Frog Skin or Duck Hunter Camouflage 1942
In 1942, the USMC approved reversible camouflage uniforms which were extensively used in the Pacific theatre of WWII. The camouflage uniforms were reversible with a green side and a brown side. In WWII, there was a one piece uniform, jacket, trousers, and helmet cover. This pattern is also popular with hunters and is commonly known as Duck Hunter pattern although this name is more appropriate for a later pattern.

In the 1950s, the United States supplied the Frog Skin pattern to France who issued it to their 1st Foreign Parachute Regiment and 2nd Foreign Parachute Regiment during the First Indo-china War. Pictures of SEAL Teams from 1963 show them wearing Frog Skin Jungle pattern (a.k.a., green duck hunter). Korean forces also used the US Frog Skin camouflage in Vietnam.

US 1942 Frog Skin Beach Pattern
Brown variant is a pale brown base with overlapping spots in three colors: khaki, mid brown, and dark brown. This was intended for beaches and arid areas.

Painting Frog Skin Jungle Patterns

Color	Color	Vallejo Model Color	Item
	Pale Green	50% Green Grey 70.886 & 50% Stone Grey or use Pastel Green 70.885	Base Color
	Earth Brown	Flat Earth 70.983 or English Uniform 70.921	Small Spots
	Green	Luftwaffe Camo Green 70.823 or Camouflage Olive Green 70.894	Medium Spots
	Brown	Chocolate Brown 70.872, Leather Brown 70.871, or German Cam Medium Brown 70.826	Large Spots

Painting Frog Skin Beach Patterns

Color	Color	Vallejo Model Color	Item
	Pale Brown	Mix Cork Brown 70.843 with Stone Grey 70.884 to get a Pale Brown 70.885	Base Color
	Earth Brown	Flat Earth 70.983 or English Uniform 70.921	Small Spots
	Beige Brown	Beige Brown 70.875	Medium Spots
	Brown	Chocolate Brown 70.872, Leather Brown 70.871, or German Cam Medium Brown 70.826	Large Spots

This method is the same for both colorways:

1. **Paint the Uniform Base Color.** Paint the uniform with a coat of the base color. This is a pale green for the jungle version or a pale brown for the beach version Add highlights by mixing 50 percent base color and 50 percent Stone Grey 70.884 to get the highlight shade. A more subtle shading can be achieved by wet blending the stone grey into the base color directly onto the figure. Note: The background for the camouflage should be lighter than when you highlight the standard uniform.

2. **Paint the Small Spots.** Paint the small spots in an earth brown color.

3. **Paint the Medium Spots.** Paint the medium spots. These are dark green on the jungle pattern and pale brown on the beach version.

4. **Paint the Large Spots in Dark Brown.** Paint large spots in a dark brown color. These overlap onto the previous spots.

2.3.2 British Windproof & Denison Smocks 1944

The French in Indochina received some garments from British stocks. These were the Denison airborne smock and the 1944 windproof jacket and trousers. The patterns were slightly different on each garment but consisted of roughly equal parts pale brown base color, green shapes, and brown shapes.

Base Color	Windproofs - Mix Cork Brown 70.843 with Stone Grey 70.884 to get a pale brown.
Base Color	Denison Smock – Iraqi Sand 70.819
Brown Shapes	Chocolate Brown 70.872, Leather Brown 70.871, German Cam Med Brown 70.826
Green shapes	Luftwaffe Camo Green 70.823 or Russian Green 70.894

1. **Paint the Uniform Base Color.** Paint the uniform with a coat of the base color. This is a pale brown for Windproofs or sand for Denison. Add highlights by mixing 50 percent base color and 50 percent Stone Grey 70.884 to get the highlight shade. A more subtle shading can be achieved by wet blending the stone grey into the base color directly on the figure. Note: The background for the camouflage should be lighter than when you highlight the standard uniform.

2. **Paint the Dark Green Shapes.** These green shapes are broad stripes and triangular forms with curved edges. These shapes cover one third of the garment. Choose a military green such as Luftwaffe Camo Green 70.823 or Russian Green 70.894.

3. **Paint the Brown Shapes.** The green shapes are broad stripes in triangular forms with curved edges. These shapes cover one third of the garment. Choose a dark brown such as Chocolate Brown 70.872, Leather Brown 70.871, or German Cam Med Brown 70.826.

British Airborne Denison Smock

2.3.3 French Lizard Pattern 1947

The lizard pattern was first used by the French Army on uniforms from 1947. It was based on the British paratroopers' Denison smock. The pattern consists of an olive-green cloth overprinted with mostly horizontal stripes of red brown and dark green.

Painting French Lizard Patterns

Color	Color	Vallejo Model Color	Item
	Pale Green	50% Green Grey 70.886 & 50% Stone Grey or use Pastel Green 70.885	Base Color
	Beige Brown	Beige Brown 70.875 or Calvary Brown 70.818	Brown Stripes
	Green	Luftwaffe Camo Green 70.823 or Camouflage Olive Green 70.894	Green Stripes

1. **Paint the Uniform Pale Green.** Paint the uniform with a coat of the base color, Green Grey 70.886. Mix 50 percent base color and 50 percent Stone Grey 70.884 to get the highlight shade. A more subtle shading can be achieved by wet blending the stone grey into the dark green directly on the figure. Note: The background for the camouflage should be lighter than when you highlight the standard uniform.

2. **Paint the Dark Green Stripes**. The stripes vary in width and are set at an angle. These stripes are painted Luftwaffe Camo Green 70.823 or Russian Green 70.894. The method is paint a dash, turn the figure, then paint another dash which joins the first one, to build up jagged stripes.

3. **Paint the Red Brown Stripes.** The stripes vary in width and are set at an angle. These stripes are painted Cavalry Brown 70.818 or Beige Brown 70.875. The method is to paint a dash, turn the figure, then paint another dash which joins the first one to build up jagged stripes.

2.3.4 Mitchell Vine Leaf Camouflage 1953

The Mitchell pattern helmet cover became a very recognizable symbol of the Vietnam War. The helmet covers were worn by US Army and USMC, AVRN, Korean, and Thai soldiers. With the onset of the Vietnam War, most US and Allied soldiers were issued camouflage helmet covers which were reversible. One side had a brown dappled pattern which is often called cloud camouflage, and the other side was printed with the Vine Leaf pattern of green leaves and a few brown twigs.

Initially developed for the USMC in 1953, the pattern was only manufactured in bulk for helmet covers and shelter quarters. Test garments such as M65 pattern jackets were developed but these were very rare. Many items were custom made using cloth cut from the shelter quarters. However, the waterproof tent fabric was heavy and hence uncomfortable for apparel.

Painting Mitchell Vine Leaf Camouflage

Color	Color	Vallejo Model Color	Item
	Pale Green	50% Green Grey 70.886 & 50% Stone Grey or use Pastel Green 70.885	Base Color
	Bright Green	German Camo Bright Green 70.833	Bright Green leaves
	Green	Luftwaffe Camo Green 70.823 or Camouflage Olive Green 70.894	Dark Green leaves
	Brown	Chocolate Brown 70.872, Leather Brown 70.871, or German Cam Medium Brown 70.826	Twigs
	Orange Brown	Beige Brown 70.875 or Orange Brown 70.981	Small Brown leaves

1. **Paint the Helmet Base color.** Paint the uniform with a coat of the base color, Green Grey 70.886. Mix 50 percent base color and 50 percent Stone Grey 70.884 to get the highlight shade

2. **Paint the Twigs.** Using a small brush, paint twigs as Y shapes using Chocolate Brown 70.872, Leather Brown 70.871, or German Cam Med Brown 70.826

3. **Paint Bright Green Leaves.** Build up the leaves with dots of German Camo Bright Green 70.833

4. **Paint Dark Green Leaves.** Build up the leaves with dots of Luftwaffe Green 70. 823

5. **Paint Brown Leaves.** Paint the small spots or leaf shapes in Orange Brown 70.981

2.3.5 Mitchell Cloud Camouflage 1953

The brown cloud side of the US Army helmet cover was rarely used in Vietnam. However, there are several photos of USMC troops at Khe Sanh wearing the helmet cover brown side out.

The same pattern was adopted by South Vietnam National Police and their American advisors. Various patterns of uniform jackets, shirts, and trousers were made in cloud camouflage.

Painting Mitchell Cloud Camouflage

Color	Color	Vallejo Model Color	Item
	Sand	Iraqi Sand 70.819	Sand base color
	Earth Brown	Tan Earth 70.874 or Flat Earth 70.983	Spots
	Khaki Brown	English Uniform 70.921 or US Tan Earth 70.874	Spots
	Beige Brown	Beige Brown 70.875	Spots
	Brown	Chocolate Brown 70.872, Leather Brown 70.871, or German Cam Medium Brown 70.826	Spots

South Vietnamese National Police in Mitchell Cloud camouflage. 28mm figure by Gringo 40s, painted by Andy Singleton.

1. **Paint the Uniform Sand.** Paint the uniform and bush hat with a coat of the base color, Iraqi Sand 70.819. Mix 50 percent base color and 50 percent Stone Grey 70.884 to get the highlight shade. Note: The background for the camouflage should be lighter than when you highlight the standard uniform.

2. **Paint Spots.** Paint the small spots in an earth brown color. Repeat with a medium brown. The spots overlap onto the previous spots. Repeat again with dark brown. The spots overlap onto the previous spots.

2.3.6 Beo Gam Vietnamese Leopard Spot 1957

The first US Special Forces soldiers in Vietnam arrived in 1957 and trained ARVN Commandos in Nha Trang from 1957 onward. These units wore commercial Duck Hunter camouflage clothing. Soon afterwards, the Vietnamese started producing their own version called Beo Gam. (beo đốm is Vietnamese for leopard spot). ARVN forces gradually changed to Tiger Stripe from about 1964 onward.

Duck Hunter camouflage shirt worn by American special forces (green berets) and was made by a Hong Kong Tailor. (Geoff Liebrandt)

This duck hunter camouflage hat was worn by an American SF advisor attached to an ARVN SF unit. (Geoff Liebrandt)

During the Vietnam War, the US and Australian Special Forces supplied Beo Gam to the Montagnard for their guerrilla warfare activities. Pictures from 1963 to 1965 show Montagnard in Bao Gam uniforms and M1 Carbines. Pictures from about 1966 onward show the majority wearing Tiger Stripe.

This pattern is slightly different to the US Frog Skin pattern in that the dots never overlap. The pattern usually has a sand colored background, but Korean soldiers had a version with a pale green background.

Color	Color	Vallejo Model Color	Item
	Sand	Iraqi Sand 70.819	Sand base color
	Earth Brown	Flat Earth 70.983 or English Uniform 70.921	Small Spots
	Green	Luftwaffe Camo Green 70.823 or Camouflage Olive Green 70.894	Medium Spots
	Brown	Chocolate Brown 70.872, Leather Brown 70.871, or German Cam Medium Brown 70.826	Large Spots

1. **Paint the Uniform Sand.** Paint the uniform and bush hat with a coat of the base color, Iraqi Sand 70.819. Mix 50 percent base color and 50 percent Stone Grey 70.884 to get the highlight shade. A more subtle shading can be achieved by wet blending the stone grey into the dark green directly on the figure. Note: The background for the camouflage should be lighter than when you highlight the standard uniform.

2. **Paint Small Brown Spots.** Paint the small spots in an earth brown color. Do not overlap the spots.

3. **Paint Small Green Spots.** Paint small spots in a military green color. Do not overlap the spots.

4. **Paint the Large Spots in Dark Brown.** Paint large spots in a dark brown color. Do not overlap the spots.

2.3.7 Tiger Stripe Camouflage 1964

Tiger Stripe camouflage was developed in Vietnam and adopted by South Vietnamese elite forces from about 1964 onward.

USMAAG advisors were authorized to wear Vietnamese camouflage uniforms but retain their US insignia. Later the Tiger Stripe pattern was also adopted by US Marine Recon, Green Berets, LRRPs, SEALs, and other elite forces. The pattern was never issued by the US government but was bought by individuals and units from commercial sources. Cloth and garments were produced in Vietnam, Thailand, Korea, and Japan, so there was a wide variation in the patterns and garments.

Pictures from 1965 to 1968 often show special forces in Tiger Stripe. Pictures from late 1968 to 1971 show tiger stripe and ERDL uniforms worn side by side and even mixing jackets and trousers.

There are many variations in color and width of the stripes. All the tiger patterns have black stripes like paint brush strokes which run horizontal when the soldier is standing. The most common form of the pattern has a pale green base color, and this is referred to by collectors as Silver Tiger. There is a later variation where the brown color is more noticeable, and this is called Gold Tiger.

There are so many variations of colors and stripes that there is at least one book dedicated to cataloguing the variants for militaria collectors.

A South Vietnamese Marine Corps (VNMC) tiger stripe shirt and beret. (Geoff Liebrandt)

Painting Tiger Stripe Camouflage

Color	Color	Vallejo Model Color	Item
	Pale Green	50% Green Grey 70.886 & 50% Stone Grey or use Pastel Green 70.885	Base Color
	Black	German Dk Grey 70.995	Black Stripes
	Earth Brown	Tan Earth 70.874 or Flat Earth 70.983	Brown Stripes on "golden tiger stripe"
	Green	Luftwaffe Camo Green 70.823 or Camouflage Olive Green 70.894	Green Stripes

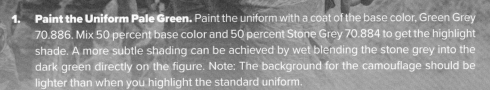

Montagnards or Degars training with US Army Rangers in 1967 Note that the instructor's jacket has pale green background and widely spaced stripes. The student has narrower spacing of the black stripes and brown stripes among the background colors. (US Military)

1. **Paint the Uniform Pale Green.** Paint the uniform with a coat of the base color, Green Grey 70.886. Mix 50 percent base color and 50 percent Stone Grey 70.884 to get the highlight shade. A more subtle shading can be achieved by wet blending the stone grey into the dark green directly on the figure. Note: The background for the camouflage should be lighter than when you highlight the standard uniform.

2. **Paint the Black Stripes.** The stripes vary in width and are slightly wavy. These stripes are painted in German Dark Grey 70.995. The method is to paint a dash, turn the figure, and then paint another dash which joins the first one.

3. **Paint the Green Stripes.** The original pattern has thin green stripes that run between the black stripes. These are quite subtle and can be ignored on small figures.

4. **Paint the Brown Stripes.** The original pattern has thin pale brown stripes that run between the black stripes. These are quite subtle and can be ignored on small figures. On larger figures paint these using a similar method to the black stripes above.

2.3.8 ERDL Camouflage 1967

The ERDL camouflage uniforms where original issued in 1967 to Pathfinders, Long Range Reconnaissance Patrol (LRRP's) members, and scout/recon teams. Later, it was issued to MACV airborne advisory and ranger advisory personnel in addition to some Special Forces personnel.

For US Forces, ERDL was issued in both green and brown dominant (depending on the intended terrain). However, this was later standardized to the green variant to simplify the supply chain. USMC combat troops wore green dominant ERDL by late 1969.

ERDL Highland

The ERDL pattern shown with the pattern repeats and shapes is the Highland version and has a sand base color. Depicted is a US battle dress jacket and trousers in the ERDL Highland Colorway.

Color	Color	Vallejo Model Color	Item
	Sand	Iraqi Sand 70.819	Sand base color
	Beige Brown	Beige Brown 70.875 or Cavalry Brown 70.818	Brown Amoeba Shapes
	Green	Luftwaffe Camo Green 70.823 or Camouflage Olive Green 70.894	Green Amoeba Shapes
	Black	German Dk Grey 70.995	Black Squiggle Shapes

ERDL Jungle

The ERDL pattern shows the pattern repetition and shapes. This is the Jungle version and has a pale green base color. Depicted is a US battle dress jacket and trousers in the ERDL Jungle Colorway.

Biet Dong Quan "Commando" Camouflage 1968

From about 1968, ERDL was also used by ARVN paratroopers, rangers, and cavalry. Period photos suggest that ARVN preferred the green variant. The Vietnamese name is Biet Dong Quan (biệt động quân = Commando)

ARVN airborne soldiers shirt in Biet Dong Quan camouflage. (Geoff Liebrandt)

ARVN Biet Dong Quan camouflage trousers. Right is the most common color, left is quite rare. (Geoff Liebrandt)

ARVN Ranger. 28mm figure by Gringo 40s, painted by Andy Singleton

Color	Color	Vallejo Model Color	Item
	Pale Green	50% Green Grey 70.886 & 50% Stone Grey or use Pastel Green 70.885	Base Color
	Beige Brown	Beige Brown 70.875 or Cavalry Brown 70.818	Brown Amoeba Shapes
	Green	Luftwaffe Camo Green 70.823 or Camouflage Olive Green 70.894	Green Amoeba Shapes
	Black	German Dk Grey 70.995	Black Squiggle Shapes

Painting ERDL and Biet Dong Quan

Base Color	Mix 50 percent Green Grey 70.886 with Stone Grey 70.884 or Pastel Green 70.885
Black Shapes	German Dark Grey 70.995.
Green Shapes	Luftwaffe Camo Green 70.823 or Russian Green 70.894
Brown Shapes	Cavalry Brown 70.818 or Beige Brown 70.875

1. **Paint the Uniform Pale Green (Jungle) or Sand (Highlands).**
    Jungle - Paint the uniform with a coat of the base color, Green Grey 70.886. Mix 50 percent base color and 50 percent Stone Grey 70.884 to get the highlight shade.

    Highland -Paint the uniform and bush hat with a coat of the base color, Iraqi Sand 70.819. Mix 50 percent base color and 50 percent Stone Grey 70.884 to get the highlight shade. A more subtle shading can be achieved by wet blending the stone grey into the dark green directly on the figure.

2. **Paint the Brown Amoeba Shapes.** The prominent feature of ERDL is brown and dark green amoeba shapes on a pale green background. Paint amorphous amoeba shapes with a red brown, such as German Camo Medium Brown 70.826.

3. **Paint the Green Amoeba Shapes.** Paint amorphous amoeba shapes with dark green, such as Luftwaffe Green 70. 823.

4. **Paint the Black Amoeba Shapes.** Paint the small black amorphous amoeba shapes with German Dark Grey 70.995.

2.4
Painting Recipes for Free World Soldiers

2.4.1 Painting 1968 USMC & US Army

Color	Color	Vallejo Model Color	Item
	Flesh	Main - Cork Brown 70.843 Shade - Flesh Wash Highlight - Flat Flesh 70.955	Face & Hands (Caucasian and Korean)
	Beige Brown	Main - Beige Brown 70.875 Shade - Flesh Wash	Face and Hands (Vietnamese, Cambodian, Laotian and Thai). Base
	Beige Brown	Main - Beige Brown 70.875 Shade - Dark Brown Wash	Face and Hands (African American, Africans). Base
	Dark Green	US Dark Green 70.893 add 50% Stone Grey 70.884 to highlight. Alternatively Green Grey 70.866 as highlight. Alternatively German Uniform 70.920	Jacket & Trousers, Cloth Cap
	Khaki Green	Russian Uniform 70.924 or US Dark Green 70.893	Pouches and backpack
	Pale Green	50% Green Grey 70.886 & 50% Stone Grey or use Pastel Green 70.885	Helmet Cover Base Color
	Black	German Dk Grey 70.995 then black wash	Boots - all over for leather boots. Jungle boots have black foot area and Green side panels. Weapon - M16 assault rifle stock & foregrip, M60 Machine gun.
	Steel	75% German Dark Grey 70.995 & 25% Silver or Gunmetal 70.863 Highlight - light drybrush of Silver	Barrel of all weapons. Magazine and Mechanism assault rifles
	Olive Grey	Khaki Grey 70.880.	Flak Jacket
	Beige Brown	Main - Beige Brown 70.875 Shade - Dark Brown Wash	Rifle Stock and foregrip (AK47 / SMD / SLR / M1 Garand / M1 Carbine / M14)
	Bright Green	German Camo Bright Green 70.833	Helmet Cover Bright Green Leaves
	Khaki Brown	English Uniform 70.921 or US Tan Earth 70.874	M79 Ammo Bandoleer
	Green	Luftwaffe Camo Green 70.823 or Camouflage Olive Green 70.894	Helmet Cover Dark Green Leaves
	Brown	Chocolate Brown 70.872, Leather Brown 70.871, or German Cam Medium Brown 70.826,	Helmet Cover Twigs
	Beige Brown	Beige Brown 70.875 or Orange Brown 70.981	Helmet Cover Small Brown leaves
	Khaki Beige	Khaki 70.988 or German Camo Beige 70.821	Rifle Sling
	Brass	Brass 70.801	Brass on Ammo Belts, ejected cartridges

28mm US army dog handler from Gringo 40s, painted by Andy Singleton

In the scales used for wargaming, there is very little difference in painting US Army and USMC. Both shared the same helmets, uniforms, weapons, and other equipment. There were differences in certain items such as flak jackets.

1. **Prepare the Figure.** Follow the steps in 2.1.1 to 2.1.5 to prepare the figure. Clean the figure and mount it on a base. Prime in black. Overbrush with white. Paint the flesh and paint the base brown.

2. **Paint the Uniform Dark Green.** Paint the base coat of the uniform with US Dark Green 70.893.

3. **Shade the Clothing.** Add highlights with Green Grey 70.886, leaving much of the US Dark Green visible in the recesses. Alternatively, mix 50 percent base color and 50 percent Stone Grey 70.884 to get the highlight shade. A more subtle shading can be achieved by wet blending the stone grey into the dark green directly on the figure.

4. **Paint Helmet Cover Green Grey.** Give the helmet cover a base color of Green Grey 70.886, or the 50:50 mix from the previous step.

5. **Paint the Black Parts.** Paint the rifle, binoculars, and boots with a very dark grey color, German Dark Grey 70.995. True black will be added later using a wash. Note that the sniper rifle had a black barrel and sight but a wooden stock.

    If you wish to emphasize the metal parts, mix some metallic silver with the dark grey and paint highlights on the weapons.

6. **Paint the Dark Brown Parts.** Using the using German Camo Medium Brown 70.826, paint the wooden parts of the sniper rifle.

7. **Paint the Flak Jacket.** Paint the Flak Jacket with Khaki Grey 70.880.

8. **Paint the Helmet Cover.** The USMC were issued camouflage helmet covers which were reversible. One side had a brown dappled pattern, and the other side was printed with the Mitchell pattern of green leaves and a few brown twigs.

    Using a small brush, paint twigs as Y shapes using German Camo Medium Brown 70.826. Build up the leaves with dots of Luftwaffe Green 70. 823 and German Camo Bright Green 70.833. Later, this was all dulled down with an olive-green wash.

9. **Paint the Eyes (optional).** Paint the eyes with a white horizontal dash and a black dot. This will give oversized and slightly misshapen eyes. Then form correct eye shapes by painting the flesh color above and below the eye. It should be noted that the eyes are only visible if you pick up the figure, so this step is not fully necessary.

10. **Shading with Washes.** Next, apply washes to emphasize the shading. Citadel Shade colors from Games Workshop are good but need a little practice. Sometimes wash effects can be quite heavy, so in each case do an experiment first and, if needed, dilute the shade with water or acrylic Matt Medium to ensure that the shading is subtle enough.
    *   Give Caucasian flesh a wash of Reikland Fleshshade.
    *   Wooden parts were washed with dark brown Agrax Earthshade.
    *   Give the uniform greens a wash of Athonian Camoshade or, if you prefer, a blue green tint using Coelia Greenshade.
    *   Shade black parts with Nuln Oil.

US Army patrol taking suspected Viet Cong for questioning. (US Military)

Graffiti on the front of Animal Mother's helmet

Graffiti on the front of Joker's helmet

Graffiti on the front of Eightball's helmet

Graffiti on the front of Charlie Sheen's helmet

< *This spectacular terrain depicts a small portion of the battle of Hamburger Hill and is based on the film.*

2.4.2 Film Characters
There are several 28 mm figures representing characters from famous films.

Full Metal Jacket - Empress Miniatures make six characters (Joker (Matthew Modine), Cowboy (Arlis Howard), Eightball (Dorian Harewood), Animal Mother (Adam Baldwin), Gunnery Sergeant Hartman (R. Lee Ermey) and Private Leonard 'Gomer Pyle' Lawrence (Vincent D'Onofrio).

Apocalypse Now - Empress make the PBR boat crew – Captain Benjamin L Willard (Martin Sheen), Chief Phillips (Albert Hall), Jay "Chef" Hicks (Frederic Forrest), surfer Lance B Johnson (Sam Bottoms), and Tyrone "clean" Miller (Larry Fishburne). Giants in Miniature have Lieutenant Colonel Kilgore (Robert Duvall). The Assault Group make the photojournalist (Denis Hopper).

Platoon - Giants in Miniature have Sergeant Elias Burns (Willem Dafoe) and Private First Class Chris Noble (Charlie Sheen) from Platoon.

Rambo - The Assault Group make Rambo (Silvester Stallone) with an M60.

Character Details
The film characters have been sculpted to match their combat attire in the second half of the film.
- Animal Mother has a red card at the right in his helmet rubber strap and bullets at the back. He has "I am become death" written in black marker on the front of the helmet.
- Cowboy has a confederate flag on the right side of his helmet.
- Eightball has insect repellent on both sides of his helmet and a drawing of an "8" pool ball on the front of his helmet.
- Joker has a circular peace badge on his chest. He has "Born to Kill" written in black marker on the front of his helmet and RTD 7-12-68 on the right side.

Sergeant Elias Burns and Private First Class Chris Noble from Platoon. Lieutenant Colonel Bill Kilgore from Apocalypse Now. Figures by Giants in Miniature from Wargames Illustrated.

Diorama by Bernard Kempinski based on Full Metal Jacket using 28mm Rubicon figures. Note that the tank is a M41 Walker Bulldog as used in the film rather than an M48 A3 as used by USMC in 1968. The film actors used US Army buttpacks instead of USMC backpacks.

Gunnery Sergeant Hartman and Private Leonard 'Gomer Pyle' Lawrence, by Empress Miniatures.

Animal Mother, Cowboy,
Eightball, and Joker,
by Empress Miniatures.

2.4.3 Painting US Special Forces

This includes Recon LRRP, MACV SOG, and SEALs as well as Montagnard and Kit Carson.

Color	Color	Vallejo Model Color	Item
	Flesh	Main - Cork Brown 70.843 Shade - Flesh Wash Highlight - Flat Flesh 70.955	Face & Hands (Caucasian and Korean)
	Beige Brown	Main - Beige Brown 70.875 Shade - Flesh Wash	Face and Hands (Vietnamese, Cambodian, Laotian and Thai). Base
	Beige Brown	Main - Beige Brown 70.875 Shade - Dark Brown Wash	Face and Hands (African American, Africans). Base
	Dark Green	US Dark Green 70.893 add 50% Stone Grey 70.884 to highlight. Alternatively Green Grey 70.866 as highlight. Alternatively German Uniform 70.920	Jacket & Trousers, Cloth Cap
	Denim Blue	Denim Blue	SEALS wearing jeans
	Black	German Dk Grey 70.995 then black wash	Boots - all over for leather boots. Jungle boots have black foot area and Green side panels. Weapon - M16 assault rifle stock & foregrip, M60 Machine gun.
	Beige Brown	Main - Beige Brown 70.875 Shade - Dark Brown Wash	Rifle Stock and foregrip (AK47 / SMD / SLR / M1 Garand / M1 Carbine / M14)
	Khaki Green	Russian Uniform 70.924	Pouches and backpack
	Khaki Brown	English Uniform 70.921 or US Tan Earth 70.874	M79 Ammo Bandoleer
	Khaki Beige	Khaki 70.988 or German Camo Beige 70.821	Rifle Sling
	Gold	Gold 70.996	Brass on Ammo Belts, ejected cartridges

US Special Forces used camouflage from about 1942 onwards. In Vietnam, the first trainers arrived in 1957 wearing US WWII Frogskin pattern which was commercially manufactured for hunting and hence commonly called Duckhunter camouflage. Pictures show Seals wearing green Frogskin in 1962. The South Vietnamese produced their own dot camouflage which was called Beo Gam, which means Leopard Spot. From about 1964, the South Vietnamese produced Tiger Stripe camouflage, and this was also adopted by trainers and US Special Forces. In 1967, the US Army issued their first woodland camouflage called ERDL. This went to LRRP units in 1967 and became very common among US and ARVN elite soldiers from 1968 onward. There was considerable overlap in the patterns, and it was also common to see mixed patterns in a unit. It was also common to see trousers in one pattern and jackets in another.

MACV SOG from Gringo 40s

- 1942 – 1963 Frogskin camouflage
- 1957 – 1964 Beo Gam (Vietnam made dot camouflage)
- 1964 – 1975 Tiger Stripe
- 1967 – 1975 ERDL

Montagnard soldiers are depicted with olive green uniforms or Beo Gam from about 1963 and Tiger Stripe from about 1966. Kit Carson scouts are shown in olive green uniforms or camouflage appropriate to the period.

US Navy Seals frequently wore American blue jeans. Denim was tougher than the lightweight tropical uniforms.

LRRP by Empress Miniatures

SEALS by Empress Miniatures

*MACV SOG by Empress
Miniatures*

2.4.4 Painting Recipe for 1954 French Troops

Color	Color	Vallejo Model Color	Item
	Flesh	Main - Cork Brown 70.843 Shade - Flesh Wash Highlight - Flat Flesh 70.955	Face & Hands (Caucasian and Korean)
	Beige Brown	Main - Beige Brown 70.875 Shade - Dark Brown Wash	Face and Hands (African American, Africans). Base
	Dark Green	US Dark Green 70.893 add 50% Stone Grey 70.884 to highlight. Alternatively Green Grey 70.866 as highlight. Alternatively German Uniform 70.920	Jacket & Trousers, Cloth Cap
	Khaki Green	Russian Uniform 70.924	Pouches & water bottle cover
	Black	Main & Shade - Black 70.950 Highlight - German Dk Grey 70.995	Boots
	Beige Brown	Main - Beige Brown 70.875 Shade - Dark Brown Wash	Rifle Stock and foregrip (AK47 / SMD / SLR / M1 Garand / M1 Carbine / M14)
	Khaki Beige	Khaki 70.988 or German Camo Beige 70.821	Rifle Sling
	Gold	Gold 70.996	Brass on Ammo Belts, ejected cartridges
	Khaki Brown	English Uniform 70.921 or US Tan Earth 70.874	M79 Ammo Bandoleer
	Khaki Beige	Khaki 70.988 or German Camo Beige 70.821	Rifle Sling
	Gold	Gold 70.996	Brass on Ammo Belts, ejected cartridges

French Troops in 1946 were equipped with US and British equipment and uniforms.
- US Frogskin camouflage jackets and trousers.
- British camouflage windproof jacket and trousers.
- Olive green jackets and trousers.
- Sand colored uniforms.
- French Lizard pattern uniforms from about 1950
- US M1 helmets or French Bush hats. French Foreign Legion (FFL) had Kepis
- US weapons – M1 Carbine, M1 Garand, Bren Gun

Step by Step Painting Guide

1. **Prepare the figures.** Following the steps in 2.1.1 to 2.1.5 prepare the figure. Clean the figure, mount it on a base. Prime in Black. Overbrush with white. Paint the flesh and paint the base brown.

2. **Paint the Uniform and Helmet.** Paint the shirt, trousers and bush hat were given a coat of the uniform color US Dark Green 70.893. Add highlights to the uniform by mixing in add 50% Stone Grey 70.884 to highlight. Alternatively follow the camouflage recipes in section 2.3

3. **Paint the Brown Parts.** Paint the wood with Beige Brown 70.875.

4. **Paint the Black Parts.** Paint the metal parts of the rifle and sub machine gun and boots with a very dark grey color,. True black will be created later using a wash. To emphasize the metal parts, mix some metallic silver with the dark grey and paint highlights on the

weapons.

5. **Paint the pouches etc.** If you want more variety, you can paint the pouches, gaiters and webbing with Russian Uniform 70.924 or Green Grey 70.886 to simulate different colors of Blanco.

6. **Paint the Eyes (optional).** Paint the eyes were painted with a white horizontal dash and a black dot. This will give oversized and slightly misshapen eyes. Then form correct eye shapes by painting the flesh color above and below. It should be noted that the eyes are only visible if you pick up the figure, so this step is not needed.

28mm French by Empress miniatures

2.4.5 Painting Recipe for 1966 Australian ANZAC

Color	Color	Vallejo Model Color	Item
	Flesh	Main - Cork Brown 70.843 Shade - Flesh Wash Highlight - Flat Flesh 70.955	Face & Hands (Caucasian and Korean)
	Khaki Green	Russian Uniform 70.924. Alternatively German Uniform 70.920. Mix with Stone Grey Stone Grey 70.884 to highlight	Uniform
	Khaki Green	Russian Uniform 70.924	Pouches and backpack
	Black	Main & Shade - Black 70.950 Highlight - German Dk Grey 70.995	Boots
	Beige Brown	Main - Beige Brown 70.875 Shade - Dark Brown Wash	Rifle Stock and foregrip (AK47 / SMD / SLR / M1 Garand / M1 Carbine / M14)
	Khaki Brown	English Uniform 70.921 or US Tan Earth 70.874	M79 Ammo Bandoleer
	Khaki Beige	Khaki 70.988 or German Camo Beige 70.821	Rifle Sling
	Gold	Gold 70.996	Brass on Ammo Belts, ejected cartridges
	Khaki Brown	English Uniform 70.921 or US Tan Earth 70.874	M79 Ammo Bandoleer
	Khaki Beige	Khaki 70.988 or German Camo Beige 70.821	Rifle Sling
	Gold	Gold 70.996	Brass on Ammo Belts, ejected cartridges

The acronym ANZAC comes from the First World War and stands for Australian and New Zealand Army Corps. The ANZAC forces supported the US Army and South Vietnamese. In August 1966, a company of 100 men were ambushed on a rubber plantation at Long Tan in South Vietnam. This battle is depicted in the film Danger Close.

These figures were sculpted in 28 mm by Paul Hicks. These figures are white metal from a British wargames company called Empress Miniatures.

From period photographs and stills from the film, Danger Close, the uniform colors varied. They started as a dark olive green and faded to a paler shade. Some garments had a blue green shade and others more khaki. In all cases, the highlights were made by mixing circa 50 percent base color and 50 percent stone grey.

Step By Step

1. **Prepare the Figure.** Follow the steps in 2.1.1 to 2.1.5 to prepare the figure. Clean the figure and mount it on a base. Prime in black. Overbrush with white. Paint the flesh and paint the base brown.

2. **Paint the Uniform.** Paint the shirt, trousers, and bush hat with a coat of the uniform color. To simulate the variety of clothing shades, paint some figures with all three garments in the same color, others with hat and trousers in the same color, and still others had all three in different shades. The base was US Dark Green 70.893 or German Uniform 70.920 or Russian Uniform 70.924.

*Australians painted by
Paul Eaglestone*

*28mm Australians by
Empress miniatures
painted by Rick Forrest.*

From left to right; 1) Hat, shirt and trousers are all Russian Uniform. 2) Hat and Trousers US Dark Green and shirt Russian Uniform. 3) Hat Russian Uniform, shirt German Uniform, trousers US Dark Green. 4) Hat and trousers German Uniform and shirt Russian Uniform.

3. **Highlight the Uniform.** Highlight the shirt, trousers, and bush hat with 50 percent base color and 50 percent Stone Grey, leaving much of the base color visible in the recesses. In cool weather, this can be done by wet blending on the figure. In hot weather, mix the paints on the palette. In summer, consider using a wet palette so that the paint remains damp.

4. **Paint the Pouches.** Paint the pouches with Russian Uniform or US Dark Green and given highlights of 50 percent base color and 50 percent Stone Grey. One rifleman has a field dressing on the rifle stock which is painted in the same colors.

   If the figure has a bullet proof vest, paint this at the same time.

5. **Paint the Black Parts.** Paint the SLR rifle, M60 machine gun, and boots with a very dark grey color, German Dark Grey 70.995. True black will be created later using a wash. If you wish to emphasize the metal parts, mix some metallic silver with the dark grey and paint highlights on the weapons.

6. **Paint the Wooden Parts.** In the 1960s, the SLR rifle stock, pistol grip, carrying handle, and foregrip were all made of hardwood and were a red brown color. From the 1970s onward, new rifles had black plastic parts instead. Paint these parts with Beige Brown 70.875.

7. **Paint the Eyes (optional).** Paint the eyes with a white horizontal dash and a black dot. This will give oversized and slightly misshapen eyes. Then form correct eye shapes by painting the flesh color above and below. It should be noted that the eyes are only visible if you pick up the figure, so this step is not needed.

8. **Shading with Washes.** The next step is to apply washes to emphasize the shading. Citadel Shade colors from Games Workshop are good but need a little practice. Sometimes wash effects can be quite heavy, so in each case, do an experiment first and, if needed, dilute the shade with water or acrylic Matt Medium to ensure that the shading is subtle enough.
   - Give Caucasian flesh a wash of Reikland Fleshshade.
   - Give the uniform greens a wash of Athonian Camoshade, or, if you prefer a blue green tint, use Coelia Greenshade.
   - Shade black parts with Nuln Oil.

9. **Highlights.** Examine each figure for mistakes and, when necessary, make corrections. Highlight he uniform and some pouches with a light drybrush of Green Grey 70.886 after the wash.

10. **Finish the Figure**. Follow the instructions in 2.1.7 to add sand, decorate the base, and varnish the figure.

Australian SAS Regiment in Tiger Stripe and ERDL

2.4.6 Painting Recipe for 1968 ARVN Army, Ranger & Paratroops, & Korean Troops

Color	Color	Vallejo Model Color	Item
	Flesh	Main - Cork Brown 70.843 Shade - Flesh Wash Highlight - Flat Flesh 70.955	Face & Hands (Caucasian and Korean)
	Beige Brown	Main - Beige Brown 70.875 Shade - Flesh Wash	Face and Hands (Vietnamese, Cambodian, Laotian and Thai). Base
	Dark Green	US Dark Green 70.893 add 50% Stone Grey 70.884 to highlight. Alternatively Green Grey 70.866 as highlight. Alternatively German Uniform 70.920	Jacket & Trousers, Cloth Cap
	Black	German Dk Grey 70.995 then black wash	Boots - all over for leather boots. Jungle boots have black foot area and Green side panels. Weapon - M16 assault rifle stock & foregrip, M60 Machine gun.
	Olive Grey	Khaki Grey 70.880.	Flak Jacket
	Beige Brown	Main - Beige Brown 70.875 Shade - Dark Brown Wash	Rifle Stock and foregrip (AK47 / SMD / SLR / M1 Garand / M1 Carbine / M14)
	Bright Green	German Camo Bright Green 70.833	Helmet Cover Bright Green Leaves
	Green	Luftwaffe Camo Green 70.823 or Camouflage Olive Green 70.894	Helmet Cover Dark Green Leaves
	Brown	Chocolate Brown 70.872, Leather Brown 70.871, or German Cam Medium Brown 70.826,	Helmet Cover Twigs
	Orange Brown	Beige Brown 70.875 or Orange Brown 70.981	Helmet Cover Small Brown leaves
	Khaki Green	Russian Uniform 70.924	Pouches and backpack
	Khaki Brown	English Uniform 70.921 or US Tan Earth 70.874	M79 Ammo Bandoleer
	Khaki Beige	Khaki 70.988 or German Camo Beige 70.821	Rifle Sling
	Gold	Gold 70.996	Brass on Ammo Belts, ejected cartridges

ARVN Paratrooper. 28mm figure by Gringo 40s, painted by Andy Singleton

Most of the ARVN wore olive green uniforms.
- 1957 – 1964 Beo Gam (Vietnam made dot camouflage)
- 1964 – 1975 Tiger Stripe
- 1967 – 1975 ERDL

ARVN Marines in 1964 – Mitchel helmet cover and Tiger Stripe uniform

Step By Step

1. **Prepare the Figure.** Follow the steps in 2.1.1 to 2.1.5 to prepare the figure. Clean the figure and mount it on a base. Prime in black. Overbrush with white. Paint the flesh and paint the base brown.

2. **Paint the Uniform Dark Green.** Paint the base coat of the uniform with US Dark Green 70.893.

3. **Shade the Clothing.** Add highlights with Green Grey 70.886, leaving much of the US Dark Green visible in the recesses. Alternatively, mix 50 percent base color and 50 percent Stone Grey 70.884 to get the highlight shade. A more subtle shading can be achieved by wet blending the stone grey into the dark green directly on the figure.

4. **Paint Helmet cover Green Grey.** Give the helmet cover a base color of Green Grey 70.886, or the 50:50 mix from the previous step.

5. **Paint the Black Parts.** Paint the rifle, binoculars, and boots with a very dark grey color, German Dark Grey 70.995. True black will be added later using a wash. Note that the sniper rifle had a black barrel and sight but a wooden stock.

    If you wish to emphasize the metal parts, mix some metallic silver with the dark grey and paint highlights on the weapons.

6. **Paint the Dark Brown Parts.** Using the using German Camo Medium Brown 70.826, paint the wooden parts of the sniper rifle and the Thompson SMG.

7. **Paint the Flak Jacket.** Paint the Flak Jacket with Khaki Grey 70.880.

8. **Paint the Helmet Cover.** The USMC were issued camouflage helmet covers which were reversible. One side had a brown dappled pattern, and the other side was printed with the Mitchell pattern of green leaves and a few brown twigs.

    Using a small brush, paint twigs as Y shapes using German Camo Medium Brown 70.826. Build up the leaves with dots of Luftwaffe Green 70. 823 and German Camo Bright Green 70.833. Later, this was all dulled down with an olive-green wash.

9. **Paint the Eyes (optional).** Paint the eyes with a white horizontal dash and a black dot. This will give oversized and slightly misshapen eyes. Then form correct eye shapes by painting the flesh color above and below. It should be noted that the eyes are only visible if you pick up the figure, so this step is not needed.

10. **Shading with Washes.** Next, apply washes to emphasize the shading. Citadel Shade colors from Games Workshop are good but need a little practice. Sometimes wash effects can be quite heavy, so in each case, do an experiment first and, if needed, dilute the shade with water or acrylic Matt Medium to ensure that the shading is subtle enough.
    - Give Caucasian flesh a wash of Reikland Fleshshade.
    - Wooden parts are washed with dark brown, Agrax Earthshade.
    - Give the uniform greens a wash of Athonian Camoshade, or if you prefer a blue green tint, use Coelia Greenshade.
    - Shade black parts with Nuln Oil.

11. **Finish the Figure.** Follow the instructions in 2.1.7 to add sand, decorate the base, and varnish the figure.

2.5 Uniforms and Equipment of Communist Forces

Uniforms & Weapons

The Viet Minh began as a partisan style resistance movement during WWII. During WWII, they were supported by the American OSS, which later became the CIA. OSS Deer Team trained 100 Viet Minh to attack the Japanese Garrison at Tan Trao northwest of Hanoi in 1945. Presumably these 100 Viet Minh were equipped with US weapons.

When the Japanese surrendered in September 1945, Ho Chi Minh acted quickly to accept the Japanese surrender and declared Vietnam independent. The Japanese surrendered many of their weapons to the Viet Minh. The Viet Minh also acquired large quantities of pre-war French weapons from the previous colonial government.

The People's Republic of China and the Soviet Union formally recognized the communist Democratic Republic of Vietnam in January 1950. The Soviets supplied large quantities of arms, mostly captured German WWII weapons. These included Mp40, Kar 98K, Mg 42, and StGw44. Over time, the Soviets and Chinese also provided Soviet weapons, particularly PPSh. With the adoption of the AK-47, the Simonov SKS rifle was phased out by the Soviets.

French troops arriving in 1946 were equipped with American and British WWII equipment and uniforms. In particular they had Lee Enfield and M1917 Enfield rifles, M1 carbines, Sten Guns, Thompsons, MAC 29 LMG, and M1919 LMG. Later the French also introduced the M2 carbine and Mat49 SMG. Many of these were captured and used by the Viet Minh.

From about 1960, the Simonov SKS rifle and the identical Chinese built Type 56 carbine were distributed as military aid to many communist groups including the NVA and Viet Cong. The SKS became the primary weapon for the Viet Cong. China made the AK-47 under license from the Soviets as the Type 56 Assault Rifle. By 1964, they had distributed huge quantities of these weapons in Southeast Asia. In Vietnam, Type 56 assault rifles were issued to the NVA.
By 1968, most of the front line NVA were issued the Type 56.

The Viet Cong had a huge variety of weapons in the late 1950s. By 1963, they had captured many American supplied weapons from the ARVN, particularly M2 carbines. As supplies of Soviet and Chinese weapons become readily available, the SKS became the primary weapon for the Viet Cong.

Uniforms

Up to 1950, Viet Minh wore civilian clothing, typically the classic black pajama suit.
Viet Minh and later NVA uniforms were mostly khaki in the early part of the conflict. From about 1950, uniforms were supplied by China. The Chinese uniforms were khaki (i.e., dark beige) or light green.

From about 1965, NVA uniforms changed to dark green. Collectors describe uniforms as Reed Green or Grey Green. The green shades varied a lot, possibly due to fading but mostly due to variations in the supply chain. Blue Grey uniforms were in theory air force but reports suggest blue grey garments were occasionally worn by other forces.

Viet Cong fighter in 1968 with SKS rifle.

VC rubber sandals
(Geoff Liebrandt)

Bowls and spoons
(Geoff Liebrandt)

NVA cold weather
sleeveless padded vest
(Geoff Liebrandt)

NVA green cotton
floppy bush hat
(Geoff Liebrandt)

Black cotton rice tube
(Geoff Liebrandt)

Canteens used by NVA
(Geoff Liebrandt)

VC black cotton trousers
with elastic waistband
(Geoff Liebrandt)

VC black cotton shirt
(Geoff Liebrandt)

Insignia
NVA soldiers did not wear insignia in combat zones. During Tet, many Viet Cong wore short pieces of blue and red ribbon pinned to their sleeves near the shoulder.

Skin Tone
Vietnamese skin tone is Vallejo 70.875 Beige Brown with a wash of GW Citadel Reikland Fleshshade.

Uniform and weapons of NVA

2.6
Painting Recipes for Communist Forces

2.6.1 Painting Recipe for 1954 Viet Minh

Color	Color	Vallejo Model Color	Item
	Beige Brown	Main - Beige Brown 70.875 Shade - Flesh Wash	Face and Hands (Vietnamese, Cambodian, Laotian and Thai). Base
	Khaki	Khaki 70.988 or German Camo Beige 70.821	Chinese supplied Uniform pre 1966
	Pale Green	50% Green Grey 70.886 & 50% Stone Grey or use Pastel Green 70.885	Alternative Color for early uniform
	Blue Grey	Luftwaffe Uniform WW2 70.816	Anti-Aircraft Gunners Jacket & Trousers, Cap
	Black	Main & Shade - Black 70.950 Highlight - German Dk Grey 70.995	Boots
	Gunmetal	75% German Dark Grey 70.995 & 25% Silver or Gunmetal 70.863 Highlight - light drybrush of Silver	Barrel of all weapons. Magazine and Mechanism assault rifles
	Silver	Silver	Blade of Bayonet
	Beige Brown	Main - Beige Brown 70.875 Shade - Dark Brown Wash	Rifle Stock and foregrip (AK47 / SMD / SLR / M1 Garand / M1 Carbine / M14)
	Khaki Green	Russian Uniform 70.924	Pouches & water bottle cover
	Khaki Brown	English Uniform 70.921 or US Tan Earth 70.874	Water Bottle, Bamboo hat
	Khaki Beige	Khaki 70.988 or German Camo Beige 70.821	Rifle Sling
	Gold	Gold 70.996	Brass on Ammo Belts, ejected cartridges

Step By Step

1. **Prepare the Figure.** Follow the steps in 2.1.1 to 2.1.5 to prepare the figure. Clean the figure and mount it on a base. Prime in black. Overbrush with white. Paint the flesh and paint the base brown.

2. **Paint the Black Parts.** The AK47 rifle and sandals are painted with a very dark grey color, German Dark Grey 70.995. True black will be added later using a wash.

3. **Paint the Brown Parts.** The stock and foregrip of the AK47 were painted brown.

4. **Paint the Uniform.** The uniform and helmet were given a coat of the main color and then highlighted with a lighter color.
     Khaki – Vallejo 70.988 Khaki with highlights of Iraqi Sand 70.

5. **Paint the Chest Rig and Pouches.** The ammunition pouches and chest rig were painted Russian Uniform.

6. **Paint the Eyes (optional).** The eyes are painted with a white horizontal dash and a black dot. This gives oversized and slightly misshapen eyes. Then the correct eye shapes are formed by painting the flesh color above and below. It should be noted that the eyes are only visible if you pick up the figure, so this step is not needed.

7. **Shading with Washes.** Citadel Shade colors from Games Workshop are used for the next stage. Sometimes wash effects can be quite heavy, so in each case, an experiment is done first and, if needed, the shade is diluted with water or acrylic Matt Medium to ensure that the shading is subtle enough.
   - Hands, feet, and faces are given a red brown wash of Reikland Fleshshade.
   - Green uniforms and pouches are shaded with a dark green wash of Athonian Camoshade.
   - Black is shaded with a wash of Nuln Oil.
   - Wooden parts are washed with dark brown, Agrax Earthshade

2.6.2 Painting Recipe for 1968 Viet Cong

Viet Cong Main Force

Viet Cong are often split into the main force and local forces. Viet Cong main forces were organized as an army and could coordinate large scale attacks. Main force Viet Cong often had support weapons such as tripod mounted machine guns, recoilless guns, and mortars. They usually moved on foot. Local forces were civilians who provided information about enemy activity and guided the main force through their regions. Local forces would sometimes also initiate ambushes and plant booby traps.

1. **Prepare the Figure.** Follow the steps in 2.1.1 to 2.1.5 to prepare the figure. Clean the figure and mount it on a base. Prime in black. Overbrush with white. Paint the flesh and paint the base brown.

2. **Paint the Jacket & Pants.** Paint the base coat of the uniform Black and overbrush with black mixed with 25 percent Dark Blue Grey 70.867 or 25 percent Oxford Blue 70.807. This gives a subtle highlight to the black clothing.

3. **Paint the Bush Hat & Pouches.** Paint ammunition pouches, vest, and bush hat Russian Uniform WWII 70.924 or Khaki 70.988

4. **Paint Conical Hats.** Paint the conical rice hat Iraqi Sand 70.819 and then add some white and drybrush to bring out the texture.

5. **Paint the Black Parts.** Paint the hair, rifle, binoculars, and boots with a very dark grey color, German Dark Grey 70.995. True black will be added later using a wash. Note that the sniper rifle had a black barrel and sight but a wooden stock.

    If you wish to emphasize the metal parts, mix 75 percent German Grey 70.995 with 25 percent Aluminum and paint highlights on the weapons.

6. **Paint the Dark Brown Parts.** Using the using German Camo Medium Brown 70.826 or Beige Brown 70.875, paint the wooden parts of weapons and the canteen.

7. **Paint the Eyes (optional).** Paint the eyes with a white horizontal dash and a black dot. This will give oversized and slightly misshapen eyes. Then form correct eye shapes by painting the flesh color above and below. It should be noted that the eyes are only visible if you pick up the figure, so this step is not needed.

8. **Shading with Washes.** Next, apply washes to emphasize the shading. Citadel Shade colors from Games Workshop are good but need a little practice. Sometimes wash effects can be quite heavy, so in each case, do an experiment first and, if needed, dilute the shade with water or acrylic Matt Medium to ensure that the shading is subtle enough.
   - Give Caucasians flesh a wash of Reikland Fleshshade.
   - Wooden parts are washed with dark brown, Agrax Earthshade.
   - Give the uniform greens a wash of Athonian Camoshade, or if you prefer a blue green tint, use Coelia Greenshade.
   - Shade black parts with Nuln Oil.

9. **Finish the Figure.** Follow the instructions in 2.1.7 to add sand, decorate the base, and varnish the figure

Ruben Torregrossa made this diorama that featured on the cover of Wargames Soldiers and Strategy Magazine.

2.6.3 Painting Recipe for PAVN or NVA North Vietnamese Army 1968

NVA uniforms were mostly Khaki in the early part of the conflict and various shades of green later. Collectors describe uniforms as Reed Green or Grey Green. The green shades varied a lot, possibly due to fading but mostly due to shortages.

Blue Grey uniforms were air force in theory, but reports suggest blue grey garments were occasionally worn by other forces.

This link is a militaria company selling genuine NVA uniforms. It is quite interesting to see the variety of colors. (Thank-you to Aberlado Barbosa for finding this.)

To see a selection of genuine NVA uniforms, go to **enemymilitaria.com** and select Vietnam War, and set the filter to Uniforms & Footwear.

From the pictures, I picked three color schemes. Khaki appears to have been common in the early war period. Grey green is a similar color to American uniforms of the period. Jungle Green is very bright and is still being used.

- Khaki – Vallejo 70.988 Khaki with highlights of Iraqi Sand 70.
- Grey Green – US Dark Green 70.893 with highlights of Green Grey 70.886.
- Jungle Green – Luftwaffe Green 70. 823 with highlights of German Camo Bright Green 70.833.

Chest Rig and Canteen could be various shades of green or khaki. Vallejo Russian Uniform 70.924 or English Uniform 70. With Wash of GW Citadel Athonian Camoshade works with any of the uniform colors.

NVA, North Vietnamese Army sculpted in 28 mm by Paul Hicks. These figures are 28 mm white metal from a British wargames company called Empress Miniatures.

Color	Color	Vallejo Model Color	Item
	Beige Brown	Main - Beige Brown 70.875 Shade - Flesh Wash	Face and Hands (Vietnamese, Cambodian, Laotian and Thai). Base
	Khaki	Khaki 70.988 or German Camo Beige 70.821	Chinese supplied Uniform pre 1966
	Green	Luftwaffe Camo Green 70.823	NVA Uniform (1966 onwards)
	Blue Grey	Luftwaffe Uniform WW2 70.816	Anti-Aircraft Gunners Jacket & Trousers, Cap
	Black	Main & Shade - Black 70.950 Highlight - German Dk Grey 70.995	Boots
	Gunmetal	75% German Dark Grey 70.995 & 25% Silver or Gunmetal 70.863 Highlight - light drybrush of Silver	Barrel of all weapons. Magazine and Mechanism assault rifles
	Beige Brown	Main - Beige Brown 70.875 Shade - Dark Brown Wash	Rifle Stock and foregrip (AK47 / SMD / SLR / M1 Garand / M1 Carbine / M14)
	Khaki Green	Russian Uniform 70.924	Pouches & water bottle cover
	Khaki Brown	English Uniform 70.921 or US Tan Earth 70.874	Water Bottle, Bamboo hat
	Khaki Beige	Khaki 70.988 or German Camo Beige 70.821	Rifle Sling
	Gold	Gold 70.996	Brass on Ammo Belts, ejected cartridges
	Khaki Beige	Khaki 70.988 or German Camo Beige 70.821	Chinese made Uniform (1950 to 1965)

Step by Step

1. **Prepare the Figure.** Follow the steps in 2.1.1 to 2.1.5 to prepare the figure. Clean the figure and mount it on a base. Prime in black. Overbrush with white. Paint the flesh and paint the base brown.

2. **Paint the Black Parts.** The AK47 rifle and sandals were painted with a very dark grey color, German Dark Grey 70.995. True black will be added later using a wash.

3. **Paint the Brown Parts.** The stock and foregrip of the AK47 are painted brown.

4. **Paint the Uniform.** The uniform and helmet are given a coat of the main color and then highlighted with a lighter color.
   - *Khaki* – Vallejo 70.988 Khaki with highlights of Iraqi Sand 70.
   - *Grey Green* – US Dark Green 70.893 with highlights of Green Grey 70.886. In the photograph below, one figure has blue grey trousers.
   - *Jungle Green* – Luftwaffe Green 70. 823 with highlights of German Camo Bright Green 70.833.

28mm Empress PAVN figures painted by Ruben Torregrossa

5.   **Paint the Chest Rig & Pouches.** The ammunition pouches and chest rig were painted Russian Uniform

6.   **Paint the Eyes (optional).** The eyes are painted with a white horizontal dash and a black dot. This gives oversized and slightly misshapen eyes. Then the correct eye shapes are formed by painting the flesh color above and below. It should be noted that the eyes are only visible if you pick up the figure, so this step is not needed.

7.   **Shading with Washes.** Citadel Shade colors from Games Workshop are used for the next stage. Sometimes wash effects can be quite heavy, so in each case, an experiment is done first and, if needed, the shade is diluted with water or acrylic Matt Medium to ensure that the shading is subtle enough.
- Hands, feet, and faces, are given a red brown wash of Reikland Fleshshade.
- Green uniforms and pouches are shaded with a dark green wash of Athonian Camoshade.
- Black is shaded with a wash of Nuln Oil.
- Wooden parts are washed with dark brown, Agrax Earthshade.

2.6.4 Painting Recipe for Khmer Rouge 1970

The Khmer Rouge were communist militia in Cambodia. They were allied with the North Vietnamese Communists and Viet Cong.

The Khmer rouge took over Cambodia in 1975. The Khmer Rouge adopted a fundamentalist "year zero" approach to communism and imprisoned anybody with an education. More than one million people were killed by the Khmer Rouge between 1975 to 1979. Vietnam invaded Cambodia in December 1978, and the war continued until 1989 when the Khmer Rouge were defeated.

In the 1960s, Khmer rouge soldiers wore black pajama style uniforms like Viet Cong. They wore a distinctive check patterned scarf called a krama and black sandals. Chinese communist hats and chest rigs were also commonly worn. Most are seen armed with AK47 assault rifles with small numbers of Soviet machine guns or RPGs. After they conquered Cambodia in 1975, the soldiers changed to green uniforms.

1. **Prepare the Figure.** Follow the steps in 2.1.1 to 2.1.5 to prepare the figure. Clean the figure and mount it on a base. Prime in Black. Overbrush with white. Paint the flesh and paint the base brown.

2. **Paint the Jacket & Pants.** Paint the base coat of the uniform black and overbrush with black mixed with 25 percent Dark Blue Grey 70.867 or 25 percent Oxford Blue 70.807. This gives a subtle highlight to the black clothing.

3. **Paint the Bush Hat & Pouches.** Paint ammunition pouches, vest, and bush hat Russian Uniform WW2 70.924 or Khaki 70.988.

4. **Paint Conical Hats.** Paint the conical rice hat Iraqi Sand 70.819 and then add some white and drybrush to bring out the texture.

5. **Paint the Black Parts.** Paint the hair, rifle, binoculars, and boots with a very dark grey color, German Dark Grey 70.995. True black will be added later using a wash. Note that the sniper rifle had a black barrel and sight but a wooden stock.
    If you wish to emphasize the metal parts, mix 75 percent German Grey 70.995 with 25 percent Aluminum and paint highlights on the weapons.

6. **Paint the Dark Brown Parts.** Using the using German Camo Medium Brown 70.826 or Beige Brown 70.875, paint the wooden parts of weapons and the canteen.

7. **Paint the Eyes (optional).** Paint the eyes with a white horizontal dash and a black dot. This will give oversized and slightly misshapen eyes. Then form correct eye shapes by painting the flesh color above and below. It should be noted that the eyes are only visible if you pick up the figure, so this step is not needed.

8. **Shading with Washes.** Next, apply washes to emphasize the shading. Citadel Shade colors from Games Workshop are good but need a little practice. Sometimes wash effects can be quite heavy, so in each case, do an experiment first and, if needed, dilute the shade with water or acrylic Matt Medium to ensure that the shading is subtle enough.
   - Give Caucasian flesh a wash of Reikland Fleshshade.
   - Wooden parts are washed with dark brown, Agrax Earthshade.
   - Give the uniform greens a wash of Athonian Camoshade, or if you prefer a blue green tint, use Coelia Greenshade.
   - Shade black parts with Nuln Oil.

9. **Finish the Figure.** Follow the instructions in 2.1.7 to add sand, decorate the base, and varnish the figure.

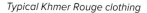

Typical Khmer Rouge clothing

2.7
Painting Recipes
for Civilians &
Livestock

2.7.1 Painting Recipe for Rural Civilians

Rural farmers traditionally wore black cotton trousers and jackets. White jackets were also common. Shirts could be white or mid blue. Women were more colorful with shirts and jackets in pink, burgundy, navy-blue, grey, red, and beige. Conical bamboo hats were very common. In Saigon, office workers wore western fashions of the time.

1.   **Prepare the Figure.** Follow the steps in 2.1.1 to 2.1.5 to prepare the figure. Clean the figure and mount it on a base. Prime in black. Overbrush with white. Paint the flesh and paint the base brown.

2.   **Paint the Jacket and Pants.** Choose suitable colors from note above and paint the jacket and trousers.

3.   **Paint the Bush Hat & Pouches.** Paint ammunition pouches, vest, and bush hat Russian Uniform WW2 70.924 or Khaki 70.988.

4.   **Paint Conical Hats.** Paint the conical rice hat Iraqi Sand 70.819 and then add some white and drybrush to bring out the texture.

5.   **Paint the Dark Brown Parts.** Using the using German Camo Medium Brown 70.826 or Beige Brown 70.875, paint the wooden parts of weapons and the canteen.

6.   **Paint the Eyes (optional).** Paint the eyes with a white horizontal dash and a black dot. This will give oversized and slightly misshapen eyes. Then form correct eye shapes by painting the flesh color above and below. It should be noted that the eyes are only visible if you pick up the figure, so this step is not needed.

7.   **Shading with Washes.** Next, apply washes to emphasize the shading. Citadel Shade colors from Games Workshop are good but need a little practice. Sometimes wash effects can be quite heavy, so in each case, do an experiment first and, if needed, dilute the shade with water or acrylic Matt Medium to ensure that the shading is subtle enough.

8.   **Finish the Figure**. Follow the instructions in 2.1.7 to add sand, decorate the base, and varnish the figure

Empress Miniatures make civilians and matching armed figures.

2.7.2 Painting Recipe for Water Buffalo

Black with cream-colored horns.

1. **Prepare the Figure.** Follow the steps in 2.1.1 to 2.1.5 to prepare the figure. Clean the figure and mount it on a base. Prime in black. Overbrush with white. Paint the flesh and paint the base brown.

2. **Paint the Body.** Paint the base coat of black and overbrush with black mixed with 20 percent Stone Grey 70.884

3. **Paint the Horns.** Paint the horns and hooves with black and overbrush with stone grey, so there is a clear contrast with the body.

4. **Finish the Figure.** Follow the instructions in 2.1.7 to add sand, decorate the base, and varnish the figure.

3D printed water buffalo. The STL files are free on the Thingiverse

Marvelous terrain pieces scratch built by Ashley Straw

Die Cast Corgi M48A3 as it comes in the box.

CHAPTER **3**

Vehicles

This chapter focuses on vehicles. Model vehicle building techniques are described using die casts, plastic models, resin models, and 3D prints. There is a comprehensive catalogue of tanks, armored personnel carriers, trucks, jeeps, boats, and helicopters.

3.1
Techniques for
Building Vehicles

3.1.1 Die Cast Vehicles

Collectible die cast vehicles are the simplest way to upgrade your forces. Simply buy the model, open the box, and play. Actually, it is not quite so simple, as suitable models only exist for a few vehicles and most of them are out of production and sought after. These items are popular on Ebay and at collector markets.

Corgi is a British manufacturer of die cast vehicles, that was founded in 1956 as Corgi Toys, a subsidiary of Mettoy. Corgi were positioned higher than other toy cars. The company was sold to Mattel in 1989, and then became independent as Corgi Classics Ltd in 1995. Corgi classics offered models from British television and also commercial vehicles in the liveries of famous companies. From 1999 to 2008, Corgi produced military aircraft and vehicles in various scales for collectors. Hornby bought Corgi Classics Ltd in 2008.

The Corgi Vietnam War collectors models remain popular, particularly the 1/50 and 1/48 scale models which match with 28 mm wargames figures. These are fully painted and weathered and feature insignia from the American forces during the Vietnam War. Unfortunately, the M151 and M113 were made in 1/43, which matches collectible diecast vehicles but not wargames.

- M48 A3 Patton Tank - 1/50 scale
- M35 Deuce Truck - 1/50 scale
- M151 Mutt (Jeep) - 1/43 scale
- M113 - 1/43 scale
- AH-1G Cobra Attack Helicopter - 1/50 scale
- Bell UH-1B Huey Helicopter – 1/50 scale

The French company, Solido, makes die cast military vehicles including a Soviet PT-76 tank in 1/48 scale, which can be repainted to serve with the PAVN. The PT-76 was used by the PAVN from 1968 to 1975.

Easy Model makes 1/72 scale collectors models including M113, M48 A3 Patton Tank, Sikorsky UH-34D, and Bell UH-1B Huey Helicopter. All of these are painted and carry insignia from the American forces during the Vietnam War.

1/48 scale models match quite well with 28 mm wargames figures. Unfortunately, there are few plastic kits in 1/48 scale vehicles. Tamiya make a Soviet T-55, which was very important for the PAVN from 1971 onward. Tamiya also make a Volkswagen Beetle and Citroen 11CV, which could be used as civilian cars in Vietnam.

There are several kits for 1/48 helicopters, but some are out of production. Hobby Boss offer a UH1 -C Huey Helicopter. Italeri offers a UH-1D Huey Helicopter, H-21C Shawnee "Flying Banana," and a Chinook CH-47 D. Revell – Monogram have made UH-1B and UH-1C Hueys and a Sikorsky UH-34D as used by the USMC.

Rubicon Models specializes in plastic kits for wargamers. Their ranges include 1/56 scale to match 28 mm wargames figures, and they already have an extensive range of WWII vehicles. Rubicon is planning to launch several variants of UH-I Huey, including UH-1D Slicks (troop carriers & medivac), Hogs (attack), and UH-1C Gunships. The first kits are due in 2022.

Building & M113 ACAV 1/72 Italeri Kit

This kit was originally created by Esci in 1987, and extra parts were added a year later to cover more variants of the vehicle. After Esci closed in 2000, the molds were purchased by Italeri. The same kit has been offered by Revell. The frames contain extra parts which enable you to build four variants. The M113 ACAV was a common armored personnel carrier in Vietnam, so this is the option that will be shown. There is also a similar kit for M106 which is the mortar carrier version of the same vehicle.

This kit has hard plastic tracks, which are constructed from 14 parts on each side. This is not difficult but does require close attention to the instructions and a good deal of patience.

Tools

You will need flush cutting clippers, tweezers, and polystyrene cement such as Revell Contacta with a brush applicator. This kit has many small dark green parts so it is a good idea to put a white paper on your cutting mat, so that you can easily see the small parts. It is also a good idea to wear reading glasses to magnify the small parts.

1. **Cut Parts from Frame.** Study the instructions and follow them step by step. Generally, it is better to only remove the parts that you need for the current step. Look closely at parts from both sides of the frame and decide where to cut them. Some are easier to cut from the front, others from the back. Put the sprue cutters flat side against the part so that the cut is straight and flush. Clean the stub with further snips and, if necessary, sand with an emery board.

2. **Wheels.** Assemble the five large road wheels to the chassis and use a flat edge to ensure that they are all vertical and flat to each other.

3. **Tracks.** Assemble the two-part wheels and sprockets taking care to align the pin on one side with the matching hole on the other side. Do not glue the rear wheel and sprocket to the chassis. Cut out the tracks for one side of the vehicle only. Leave the track parts for the other side on the frame so that you can check the part numbers. Each track part has an inside and an outside. On the single-track links, the round circle from the ejector pin is on the inside. The tracks have two broad lugs on the front side and three small lugs on the rear side. Starting with the rear sprocket in its correct orientation to the chassis, check the instructions to see which direction the track goes.

   Apply a small amount of glue on the sprocket and add the single-track link so that the

teeth of the sprocket go through the two holes in the link. Repeat until you have five links. Dry fit the long top section of track but do not glue it in place yet. Check the direction of the track from the sprocket to the long top track and then the rear wheel. Taking care to follow the same track link direction, assemble four single links to the rear wheel. Make sure that you have an even overhang on each side.

Glue the sprocket, rear wheel, and long top track piece in place and adjust them to look natural before they dry. Follow the instructions and add the remaining four parts to complete the bottom portion of the track.

Repeat these processes on the other side. Sand the track sides to remove the scabs from the sprue attachments.

4. **Interior.** The kit includes interior walls and seating that can be seen if the doors and hatches are opened. This step can be skipped if the vehicle is to be "buttoned up" with all doors and hatches closed.

5. **Exterior.** Add lights, hatches, and stored items. Decide if you want to have hatches open. If you do, it is a good idea to leave the chassis, body, and rear doors separate so that the interior can be painted before final assembly.

6. **Armament.** The ACAV version has two M60 machine guns and a M2-HB 50 Cal machine gun.
As this model is the ACAV version, gun shields are added, and the track skirts are not applied.

7. **Painting.** Mask the contact surfaces of the chassis. Spray the interior with a primer and then paint the walls in light green. Paint the floor Olive Drab and the bench tops tan earth. The central seat is black. Spray the exterior of the vehicle with Olive Drab.

Building an M48 A3 Patton Tank by Italeri in 1/72 Scale

A kit for the M48 A2 was launched by Esci in 1987. Soon after, parts were added to make other versions including the M48 A3. After Esci ceased trading, the molds were bought by Italeri. The same kit is offered by Revell.

The kit can make different versions and has separate pages of instructions according to the variant. The M48 A3 has a slightly different main gun and commander's turret and has five small support wheels for the upper side of the tracks.

The kit is quite detailed with many small parts. It is a good idea to cut parts from the sprue as you need them in the assembly sequence. Many parts look similar but have different numbers according to whether they go on the right or left side.

Step by Step

Remove Parts from Sprue
Examine each part and note how it is attached to the sprue. Find the best angle to cut and snip the parts flush cut pliers with the flat side against the part. Remove any remaining lumps from the sprue attachment with further clipper cuts. Sand or file if necessary.

Support Wheels
There are placements for three small track support wheels on each side of the hull. To make M48 A3 version, you will have to add two sets of small wheels, and there are no markings on the hull. Draw a line above the wheel lugs so that you get the vertical alignment and then mark the halfway points so the wheels are equidistant and level.

Large Wheels
The large lower track wheels have three variants so follow the instructions carefully. Cut a length of sprue and use this as a spacer so that the lower wheels are even and parallel to the top wheels.

Tracks
The kit has multi-part tracks so start at the toothed wheel and work your way round, paying careful attention to the next part number.

The 1/50 scale Corgi M48 A3 is a very dark green as used by USMC. However the decals show US Army. The 1/72 Italeri is a more typical US army color.

3.1.3 Resin Kits

Empress Miniatures offers resin and white metal kits for many vehicles, including Cadillac Gage commando, Centurion, M48 Patton, M67 Zippo, M113, Ontos, Otter, PBR boat, PT-76 T-54, and T-55.

Full Metal Miniatures offers Centurion, M41 Walker Bulldog, PBR, PT-76, and T-54

The Assault Group has a M113.

Cleaning

For the Empress Miniatures Cadillac Gage Commando Armored Car, the model has a polyurethane resin body, wheels, and turret. The hatches and machine guns are white metal.

Take a lot of time with the clean-up and dry fit. Inspect the parts and, if necessary, sand with emery boards to remove blemishes. There may be residue from the casting process on the back of the wheels and the underside of the turret.

If there are bubbles or sink marks, fill them with Milliput. In this example case, there were no areas that needed filling.

Clean up metal parts, remove silver threads from the vents, and remove scabs from the molding gates.

The axles are molded on to the body. The ends of the axles have small stubs from the casting process that can be removed with sprue cutting pliers. To ensure that the axle fits smoothly into the recess in the wheels, first measure the diameter of the axle with a Digital Vernier and select the matching size drill bit. Drill out the hole in the wheel by hand with Pin Vise.

If you break an axle, replace it with a brass rod or tube.

Dry fit all parts before assembly.

Adding Magnets

If you are going to use magnets, this is best done before anything else is attached.
A nice feature is to be able to rotate the turret and at the same time ensure that it will not fall out. To achieve this, fix a 6 mm x 2 mm diameter magnet centrally in the hull under the turret.

Assembly

The general idea is to assemble from the inside out. Start with the wheels, then the turret, and then add hatches and machine guns.

Painting

Spray with Citadel Chaos Black as primer.

Spray with Vallejo 28.003 Russian Green Spray. The color is the same as Vallejo 70.894 Camouflage Olive Green (which they used to call Russian Green a few years ago).

After spray painting, the vehicle looks brand new and very smooth. You can over-paint it and weather it to make it looked used and dirty.

Paint the tires with German Dark Grey.

Paint the machine guns with German Dark Grey mixed with Silver.

Paint the tires and machine guns with a black wash, such as Citadel Nuln Oil. This will darken the deep areas to full black and darken the corners and recesses of the deck

3.1.4 3D Printed Vehicles

3D Printing Technologies

There are two relevant 3D printing types, Fused Deposition Modelling (FDM) and Stereolithography (SLA).

Fused Deposition Modelling (FDM) uses a plastic filament that is fed through a heated nozzle mounted on a three-axis CNC positioning machine. This draws out the shape in thin layers of plastic and gradually builds up the 3D shape. FDM was the first form of 3D printing to become affordable to the home hobbyist, with machines costing less than US$500 available from about 2015 onward. The FDM process can build large models, but the construction process leaves noticeable steps on angled surfaces as each layer is added. Typical layer height can vary from fine quality 0.08 mm to draft quality 0.4 mm. If a smooth surface is required, it can take a lot of filing and sanding. There are many companies offering FDM printing models.

Stereolithography (SLA) is a much more accurate process capable of printing intricate detail and smooth surfaces. SLA was invented by Chuck Hull in 1986. These 3D printers are often described as resin printers, and all share the same principles.

Resin printers have a bath of liquid photopolymer resin with a transparent film as the base. Ultraviolet (UV) light shines from underneath the bath and through the film which cures the resin to form hard plastic layer. A build-plate, mounted on a screw lift, is lowered into the bath until it is very close to the transparent film. The first layer sticks to the plate. The screw lifts the base plate, and the next layer is drawn by the lights. This builds up layers which are typically 0.02 to 0.05 mm thick, so it takes at least 500 layers to make an object 25 mm (1 in) thick. Usually, the model is supported by a scaffold framework of printed resin. Over a period of many hours, the object is built up and hangs from the build plate. When the print is finished, the build plate rises to the top of the screw tower and is ready for removal. After printing, the model is wet with uncured resin and must be cleaned in a suitable solvent. Most resins also require post-print curing; either controlled UV lights or sitting in sunlight to ensure the resin is fully cured throughout.

Preparing FDM 3d Printed Vehicles

There are many companies which offer 3D printed models. Many of these are made by Fused Deposition Modelling (FDM) and have a very noticeable woodgrain effect from the layers.

Step by Step

Clean Up

Sand the easy to reach parts with an Emery stick (sandpaper nail file). Scrape everywhere else with a flat ended sculpting tool to remove left over filament.

Apply Filler

Apply Mr Surfaces 500 filler liquid straight from the bottle with a flat nylon brush about 6 mm wide. It goes on like thick paint and shrinks as it dries. After the first coat dries, apply some more. You will need decorators' solvent paint thinners to clean the brush afterward.

Sand again

Leave the model to dry overnight and then sand it again. Cut small slices from the emery stick to make a 5 mm x 20 mm and a 8 mm x 20 mm sanding pad to get in the awkward difficult to reach parts.

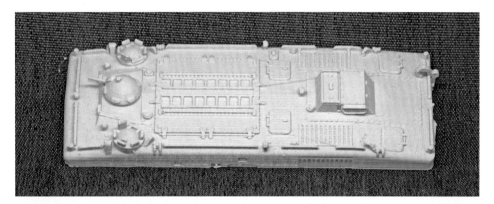

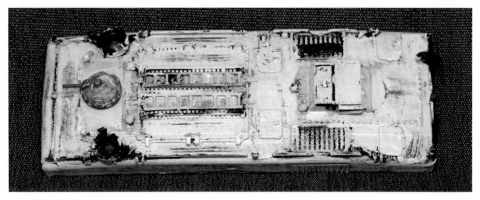

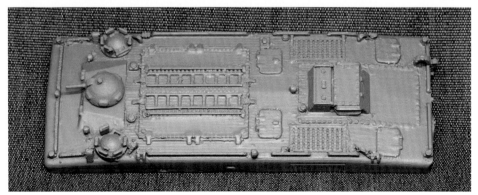

Resin Prints

Sourcing STL files

Printing high quality models requires high quality files. There are a lot of good free files that can be found; however, there are also a lot of very low-quality files. It is always worth checking that the file you are looking at is of sufficient detail for your required scale.

A good place to start is Google. Search STL with the name of the vehicle or model that you want. This will probably direct you to https://www.thingiverse.com/ or https://www.mymini-factory.com/ or a similar website. A webstore for wargaming STLs like https://wargaming3d.com/ contains both STLs for sale and relevant free files. Individual files can be expensive, so keep an eye out for Kickstarter, where there are often themed offers. Some designers are on Patreon and offer models for a monthly subscription.

Files can be created and modified using several free software suites, but that is a topic beyond the scope of this book.

Preparing the File

Prepare the file with the slicer software. This can be the software supplied with the printer or a separate software. Chutibox is free for the basic version and easy to use. If you are using a propriety software, you must set the print volume sizes and machine type in the software. It is a good idea to do a dimensional check to see if the finished print is the same dimensions that you have in the software.

If you are printing a vehicle, go to Wikipedia and check the length and width. Width is often easiest as length can be influenced by the gun barrel and height by the radio aerials. Then work out the size at the desired scale. If you want 1/50 scale, divide the real length by 50. This is easy, if you stick to metric measurements. A tank that is 9 meters (9000 mm) long in real life and is 180 mm long at 1/50 scale. In the software, note the percent scaling and then apply the same percent to the tracks, turret, cupola, and machine gun. If the files were designed to be printed at a small scale, the details may look poor if they are scaled up a long way. Similarly, a large-scale model may become very fragile if the parts are scaled down.

You can print several parts at a time, if they do not overlap. Make sure that the exposure is in the correct time to suit your resin (e.g., bottom exposure 40 seconds; normal exposure 4 seconds). Exposure times vary by resin, machine, and environment. Colder environments need longer exposure time. Check for the manufacturer's recommended times for the resin that you are using. Layer height should be 0.05 mm for standard printing or 0.03 mm for best quality. The software will tell you the expected print time which could be an hour for small thin parts up to seven or more hours for a 28 mm tank body. The software will also calculate the approximate volume of resin required.

When you master the software, you can reduce the resin quantity by making the models hollow with the outer walls 1.8 to 3.0 mm thick. You should also add two drainage holes on the underside of the model; one to let resin out and another to let air in. These need to be at least 4 mm diameter.

Angle the Model

With a resin printer, printing a straight section parallel to the FEP, such as a tank gun barrel, can cause strange effects where the print is curved or incomplete.

Many things print better if they are at an angle to the bed, as this creates natural support for the layers to build up onto each other. When you look at a wargaming tank, you focus on the top and front. If the model is at an angle with the back bottom edge close to the baseplate, the top front will have the least number of supports. This means that there is much less work to clean up the surface, and that there is less risk of disfiguring the model with stumps or pock marks when the supports are removed. However, printing flat surfaces that are set at an angle can cause a woodgrain effect from the layers. Sometimes experimentation is needed.

Print Supports

External supports are important to get a good quality print and to prevent print failures. The software will have some automatic functions to do this, but it is worth watching YouTube videos to learn where to add supports and how many. As a rule of thumb, it is always worth adding more supports around the points closest to the plate and checking to ensure that all the overhanging parts of the model are supported.

Printing

Fill the vat with resin. Standard resin is easy to print but brittle when cured. There are tough resins that are flexible, but these tend to be more expensive. Tough resin is recommended for figures with long thin weapons.

Save the sliced file to a USB stick and transfer this to the printer. Set the print running. Check after an hour and every two hours thereafter to ensure that there is enough resin and that the print is working. The pause button is useful, as this raises the printing plate so that you can see the model clearly and refill the bath.

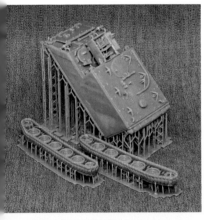

Removing the Model

You can remove the model from the base plate before or after washing. With a Wash & Cure machine it is easiest to leave the model on the base plate and wash the whole thing. Using the scraper, remove the model from the base plate and then wash it thoroughly in a suitable solvent.

Washing

The printed model will be covered in sticky resin. Standard resins need to be washed in strong alcohol. There are some water-based resins which can be washed in water.

Wearing gloves, remove build plate and the model and place it in the solvent bath. This can be a large Tupperware container with a liter of old dirty solvent. Shake gently so that the excess resin is removed. Best practice is a second wash in cleaner solvent to get the parts thoroughly clean. A wash machine with a stirrer and a mesh basket is efficient and less messy than washing by hand. Finally, wash the model in hot water with a drop of liquid soap

Removing the Supports

While the model is in hot water, the plastic supports will slightly soften. This is the best time to remove the supports. Chunky parts can be separated from their supports easily with your hands. Thin section parts, such as mudguards and gun barrels are delicate, so remove the supports using flush cutting pliers.

If the supports are difficult to remove, they may be overexposed, so reduce the exposure for the next print.

Curing

In summer, you can leave the model in the sunshine for an hour to ensure it is fully cured. If you are going to print a lot, invest in a Wash & Cure machine. The curing machine has UV lamps and a rotating turntable. It will fully cure a model in less than 5 minutes. If the model has recessed details, turn it over and repeat the cure cycle.

Sanding and Assembly

Once washed and cured, the parts may need some sanding on the underside to remove the stumps from the supports. There is usually no need to clean up the upper surfaces.

With tanks, sometimes the turret spigot does not fit easily into the corresponding recess in the hull. If this happens, use a digital caliper to measure the dimensions of the spigot and the hole. Measure both along the length and across the width of the vehicle. You can either sand down the spigot or enlarge the hole in the hull using a Dremel with a diamond rasp bit.

Assembly is very quick. Many models are printed as one piece. Even a 1/48 scale tank will only have six parts - hull, two tracks, turret, cupola, and machine gun.

Decide if you want to paint some of the parts before assembly, as this is often easier. Glue parts together with cyanoacrylate superglue. Turrets and cupolas can be fixed with magnets allowing them to be turned. This also means that you can exchange cupolas between buttoned up or crew visible scenarios. A big advantage is that, if you damage a part, you can print another one.

Painting

You can paint 3D prints in the same way as a plastic or resin model. Undercoat with either acrylic spray paint or a brush on primer such as acrylic Gesso. Paint the details using normal model acrylics such as Vallejo Model Color. Washes can also be used. Dry brushing needs to be done carefully as it tends to emphasize the woodgrain lines created by the print layers.

3.1.5 Painting & Decals

Painting

Color	Color	Vallejo Model Color	Item
	Steel	75% German Dark Grey 70.995 & 25% Silver or Gunmetal 70.863 Highlight - light drybrush of Silver	Barrel of all weapons. Magazine and Mechanism assault rifles
	Forrest Green	Green Grey 70.886, Spray Russian Green 28.003	USMC vehicles
	Khaki Green	US Olive Drab 70.887 Spray 28.005	Helicopters
	Khaki Green	Russian Uniform 70.924, Spray Russian Uniform 28.007	US Army vehicles
	Russian Green	Camouflage Olive Green 70.894, Spray Russian Green 28.003	North Vietnamese vehicles

If you are unsure of the material or if you have done a lot of sanding, wash the model and let it dry.

If you are going to paint with a brush, first spray with primer such as Citadel Chaos Black.

If you are doing a green military vehicle, you can use a spray that is both primer and color coat such as Vallejo 28.003 Russian Green Spray. This color is the same as Vallejo 70.894 Camouflage Olive Green, which they used to call Russian Green a few years ago.

After spray painting, the vehicle looks brand new and very smooth. You can over-paint it and weather it to make it looked used and dirty.

DRYBRUSH
1-2 HOUR

ZENITHAL
2-4 HOURS

COLOR MODULATION
4-8 HOURS

Ruben Torregrossa painted these 1/100 scale tanks using various techniques.

Paint the tires and metal parts of weapons with German Dark Grey 70.995. True black will be added later using a wash such as Citadel Nuln Oil.

To emphasize the metal parts, mix some metallic silver with the dark grey and paint highlights on the weapons.

There are many ways to weather vehicles.

First dilute some red-brown paint in lots of water and apply this as a wash. You can add a drop of dishwash soap to reduce surface tension, so that the brown gathers in the recesses. Allow this to dry. Apply this brown wash heavily to tires and tracks and then wipe some off with tissue paper so that the dirt is deep in the treads.

Next mix the original color with a small amount of Stone Grey to lighten it slightly and drybrush this on the flat panels. Lighten this again and drybrush carefully to highlight paned edges.

Mix silver metallic paint with German Dark Grey 70.995 and lightly drybrush the track surfaces to highlight that they are metal. Similarly, drybrush the vehicle corners to simulate wear and tear.

Decals

Plastic kits are usually supplied with waterslide decals. There are also some companies that sell decals separately. Unfortunately, the Vietnam War is a niche period, so decal companies such as Star Decals only offer Vietnam War vehicle decals in 1/72 and 1/35 scale. With care, many can be used for wargames vehicles in the 1/48 to 1/56 scales.

Decal sheets often have artwork for several variants, so it is usually best to cut out the decals that you require from the sheet.

If the surface is rough or has been heavily dry brushed, paint gloss varnish on the area which will receive the decal. Let this dry before the next step.

A decal bath is a small plastic tray with a second slotted tray inside. This is often convenient, as you can wet the decals until they start to release and then lift them out of the water before they escape from the paper.

Dampen the area that will receive the decal. Lift the decal on the release paper and slide it onto the desired position with a wet paint brush. If this is difficult apply a drop of water to help lubricate under the decal.

Once the decal is in the right place let it dry. Apply matt varnish so that the glossy effect is hidden.

3.2
Tanks

Australian Centurion tank. Rubicon kit with Eureka crew built by Gareth Ewart.

M24 Chaffee

M41 Walker Bulldog

M42 Duster by Empress Miniatures

Centurion

The Centurion was the primary British Army main battle tank (MBT) of the post-WWII period. Introduced in 1945, it remained in production into the 1960s and saw combat into the 1980s. Centurion tanks were deployed in Vietnam by the Australian forces. The main armament was a 84 mm 20 lb cannon. The Centurion weighed 52 tons and had a top speed of 22 mph and a range of 50 miles.

M24 Chaffee

The M24 was a US built light tank introduced in late 1944 to replace the M5 Stuart. It was armed with a 75 mm main gun plus a M2 HB 50 caliber machine gun and two 30 caliber M1919 machine guns. The Chaffee weighted 18 tons and had a range of 100 miles (160 km). Top speed was 35 mph (56 km/h).

The French bought 1,254 M24s after WWII, and some were deployed in Indochina. There were 10 at the Battle of Dien Bien Phu in 1954. At least 127 were bought by ARVN. By the late 1960s, spare parts were in short supply, so many were parked at defensive points around military bases. They saw action during the Tet Offensive at Hue in 1968.

M41 Walker Bulldog

The M41 was US built light tank introduced in 1951 to replace M254 Chaffee. The main armament was a 76 mm main gun, a M2 HB 50 caliber machine gun, and a coaxial 30 caliber M1919 machine gun. The tank weighed 23.5 tons and had a range of 100 miles (160 km). Top speed was 45 mph (72 km/h). The ARVN was supplied with 580 M41s between 1965_ and 1972. From 1971, the PAVN fielded large quantities of T54 tanks which outgunned the M41. In October 1974, the ARVN had 371 in total but only 197 were operational. Most were destroyed in 1975 Spring Offensive.

M42 Duster

The M42 40 mm self-propelled anti-aircraft gun, or "Duster," was an American armored light air-defense gun based on M41 Walker Bulldog tank. It was armed with twin Bofors M2A1 40 mm anti-aircraft guns. Dusters were originally sent to Vietnam to provide low level air defense. Once US had air superiority, they were repurposed for ground fire support in Vietnam and saw extensive action. The Duster weighed 24.8 tons and had a range of 100 miles (160 km). The top speed was 45 mph (72 km/h).

M48 A3 Patton Tank

The M48 Patton tank was the MBT of US forces in the 1960s. From 1959, most had been upgraded to M48 A3 specification. The M48 A3 has an upgraded 90 mm main gun with coaxial 30 Cal machine gun and commander's turret. The M48 A3 is easily identifiable, because it had five small support wheels for

25th Infantry Division M48A3 Patton moving through Viet Cong territory Operation Lincoln in 1966.

M50 Ontos by Empress Miniatures

M67 Zippo by Empress Miniatures

M551 Sheridan – 3D resin print using STL from BobMac.

the upper part the tracks, where predecessors only had three. The tank weighed 45 tons and had a range of 280 miles (460 km). The top speed was 30 mph (48 km/h).

The US deployed 600 M48s to Vietnam from 1965 onward. It was used by the US Army and USMC. As US forces reduced, many were supplied to ARVN. In total, 343 M48s were delivered to the ARVN. Many were destroyed in the 1975 Spring Offensive. At the end of the war, NVA captured about 30 M48s, most of which became war memorials.

M50 Ontos
Ontos, officially the rifle, multiple 106 mm, self-propelled M50, was a US light armored tracked anti-tank vehicle developed in the 1950s. The Ontos weighed 8.6 tons and had a range of 115 miles (185 km). The top speed was 30 mph (48 km/h).

The M50 mounted six 106 mm manually loaded M40 recoilless rifles as its main armament, which could be fired in rapid succession. It also carried a 30 caliber M1919 machine gun.

Most of the 297 produced went to the USMC. The USMC consistently reported excellent results when they used the Ontos for direct fire support against infantry during the Vietnam War. Ontos was removed from service in 1969.

M67 Zippo
Thee M67 flame thrower tank (FTT) was a flame thrower based on M48 A2 or M48 A3 MBT. It was nicknamed "Zippo" after a famous brand of cigarette lighters. The M7 flame projector fired liquid petrol up to 120 meters (490 ft). The flamethrower was mounted inside a fake gun barrel, making the vehicle look similar to a standard M48 tank. The FTT weighed 45 tons and had a range of 280 miles (460 km). The top speed was 30 mph (48 km/h). It was used by both the US Army and USMC during the Vietnam War

M551 Sheridan
M551 "Sheridan" armored reconnaissance/ airborne assault vehicle (AR/AAV) was an American light tank. It was designed to be landed by parachute and to swim across rivers. It was armed with M81/M81 Modified/M81E1 152 mm gun/launcher, which fired both conventional ammunition and the MGM-51 Shillelagh guided anti-tank missile.

The M551 tank weighed only18 tons and had a range of 350 miles (560 km). The top speed was 43 mph (70 km/h).

The M551 was rushed into combat service in Vietnam in January 1969. It was highly maneuverable but vulnerable to mines and RPGs.

XM706 Cadillac Gage Commando by Empress Miniatures

Empress Miniatures PT-76 tank built and painted by Paul Eaglestone.

Empress Miniatures T-54 tank built and painted by Paul Eaglestone

XM706 Cadillac Gage Commando

The Cadillac Gage Commando armored car was developed for the United States Military Police Corps during the Vietnam War as an armed convoy escort vehicle. The US built 3200 were in various versions. The Commando was deployed in Vietnam from 1963 onward and was used by US forces and the ARVN. ARVN versions were armed with two 30 caliber machine guns. US versions usually had two 7.62 mm NATO M73 machine guns. The XM706 weighed 8 tons and had a range of 400 miles (644 km). The top speed was 62 mph (100 km/h). It was also amphibious.

M728 Combat Engineer Vehicle

The M728 Combat Engineer Vehicle (CEV) is an American full-tracked vehicle based on the M60 MBT. Production commenced in 1965 and, by 1987, 312 of all variants were produced. A small quantity were deployed in Vietnam in 1968 and were used for fire support, base security, counter ambush fire, and direct assault of fortified positions. The main armament is a short barreled 165 mm M135 gun. The M728 could be fitted with a M9 Dozer Blade Assembly and the A-frame crane. The vehicle weighed 47 tons and had a range of 280 miles (460 km). The top speed was 30 mph (48 km/h).

Soviet PT-76 and & Chinese Type 63 Tanks

The PT-76 is a Soviet amphibious light tank and was the standard reconnaissance tank of the Soviet Army and the other Warsaw Pact armed forces. The main armament was a 76.2 mm D-56T series rifled tank gun. Its chassis served as the basis for a number of other vehicle designs, many of them amphibious, including the BTR-50 armored personnel carrier. Soviet factories made about 12,000 PT-76 tanks. The PT-76 weighed 16 tons and had a range of 275 miles (450 km). The top speed was 31 mph (50 km/h). North Vietnam received 150 Soviet PT-76s between 1959 and 1960 and 100 more Soviet PT-76s between 1971 and 1972.

The Chinese Type 63 amphibious light tank was based on the PT-76 but with a rounded turret like a T-54 rather than the truncated cone of the PT-76. The main armament was a 85 mm Type 62-85TC rifled gun. The vehicle weighed 16 tons and had a range of 210 miles (340 km). The top speed was 31 mph (50 km/h) cross country and 7 mph (12 km/h) in water. North Vietnam received 150 Chinese Type 63 tanks between 1970 and 1972.

Soviet T-54, T-55, & Chinese Type 59 Tanks

The T-54 and T-55 tanks are a series of Soviet MBTs introduced in the years following WWII. Production began in 1947 and continued for many years, with various updates every few years. The T-54/55 series eventually became the most-produced tank in history. Estimated production numbers for the series range from 86,000 to 100,000. Main armament was a 100 mm rifled tank gun with a 7.62 mm SGMT medium coaxial machine gun. There was a bow-mounted 7.62 mm SGMT medium bow mounted and many also had a 12.7 mm DShK anti-aircraft gun fitted to the turret. The T-54 weighed 36 tons and had a range of 275 miles (450 km). The top speed was 31 mph (50 km/h).

North Vietnam received 400 T-54s between 1970 and 1972 and 600 T-55s between 1973 and 1975 from the Soviet Union. The T-59 MBT is a Chinese-produced version of the Soviet T-54A tank. 10,000 were produced by China beginning in 1963. 350 T-59s delivered by China from 1970 to 1972.

Empress Miniatures T-54 tank built and painted by Paul Eaglestone.

3.3
Armored Personnel Carriers

LVTP-5 and Variants

The LVTP-5 (landing vehicle, tracked, personnel) was an armored, tracked amphibious landing vehicle. It was 30 feet (9 meters) long and 10 feet (3 meters) high, fully enclosed, and could carry 30 to 35 fully-equipped marines. The vehicle weighed 37 tons and had a range of 190 miles (306 km) on roads or 57 miles (92 km) in water. The top speed was 30 mph (48 km/h) on land and 7 mph (11 km/h) in water. The USMC made extensive use of them during the Vietnam War. The US produced 1,124 of the standard LVTP-5. There were variants including 210 of the fire support vehicle LVTH-6 (landing vehicle, tracked, howitzer) armed with M49 105 mm howitzer of which 210 were built. Sixty-five recovery vehicles LVTR-1 (landing vehicle, tracked, recovery) were built and 41 of the mine clearance vehicle LVTE-5 equipped with a dozer blade.

LVTP-5 model 3D printed and painted by Thomas Riepe

M113 Family of AFVs

The M113 was the first aluminum armored fighting vehicle (AFV) to go into mass production. This was much lighter than previous steel vehicles so could be transported by air. The vehicle could also be amphibious. A total of 80,000 were manufactured from 1960 onward, and these are known to have served in at least 70 armies worldwide. The M113 and its variants are still in service with many armies.

The first batch of 32 M113s were delivered to ARVN in March 1962. In total the ARVN received 1,635 M113 and its variants. US Armed Forces purchased 3,000 M113s in total with probably more than 2,000 M113s in service in Vietnam at any time during the conflict.

The first combat experience for M113s was in Vietnam. These vehicles had side skirts over the tracks and the 50 caliber machine gun was mounted without any gun shield to protect the gunner. During the battle of Ap Bac in January 1963, all 14 gunners were killed. As a result, the ARVN started to modify the vehicles with gun shields and turrets.

The standard vehicle weighed 12 tons and had a range of 300 miles (480 km). The top speed was 42 mph (68 km/h) on land and 3.6 mph (5.8 km/h) in water.

M113 ACAV

This version of the armored cavalry assault vehicle (ACAV) was developed during the Vietnam war, mostly in response

All M113 variants are 3D resin print using STL from BobMac. com

to casualties observed with the exposed gunner/commander and losses observed at the ambush of Ap Bac (January 2, 1963). The ACAV was at first an improvised field modification

M113 Early

American M106 and Australian M125 Mortar Carrier

M132 Armored Flamethrower

M577 Command Vehicle

by the South Vietnamese Army (ARVN) in 1963. In 1965, the ACAV kits were standardized and armor plate mass-produced in the US. The standard ACAV kit from 1965 onward was a fully circular turret armor for the commander/gunner and gun shields for the two M60 machine guns. Also, the skirts over the tracks were removed to avoid clogging up with mud. M113 ACAVs were used in large quantities by US Forces and ARVN.

American M106 and Australian M125 Mortar Carriers
The Americans deployed the M106 which was a mortar carrier armed with a 4.2 inch (106.7 mm) M30 mortar mounted on a turntable in the rear troop compartment. On this variant, the single hatch over the rear troop compartment was exchanged for a three-part circular hatch. The mortar could be fired from the vehicle but could also be fired dismounted.

Australian forces used a similar vehicle, the M125AS4 armored mortar, which was equipped with an 81 mm mortar.

M132 Armored Flamethrower
The M132 was a variant of the M113 equipped with a turret-mounted M10-8 flame gun. The flame thrower had a 200-gallon fuel capacity which enabled it to fire for up to 32 seconds, and the pressure unit enabled it to reach targets at a range of (170 meters). A total of 350 were built, and they were used by US forces and ARVN in Vietnam.

M577 Command Vehicle
The M577 was a command vehicle based on the M113. The roof over the rear troop compartment is higher than the standard version and is equipped with additional radios and a generator. A few vehicles were also used as ambulances. The M577 was used by US forces, Australian forces, and ARVN.

Australian M113 Variants in Vietnam
Australia deployed 163 x M113 A1, 11 x M113A1 Fitters (repair vehicle), 10 x M125A1 mortar Carriers, 8 M577 command vehicles, and 8 x M113A1 FSV (Fire Support Vehicle) with Saladin Turret).

M29C Weasel
During WWII, US forces used the M29c Weasel which was a small tracked vehicle carrying soldiers and supplies across terrain inaccessible by wheeled vehicles. Originally designed for snow, they were deployed in the Pacific theater including Iwo Jima and Okinawa. M29s were semi amphibious and could swim in inland waterways.

In 1947, many of these were supplied to French forces in Indochina, and they were used in the Mekong Delta area. Later French M29Cs were upgraded with a variety of machine guns and some with either 57 mm recoilless guns or 60 mm mortars. These armed vehicles were called Crabes.

M76 Otter

The M76 Otter was developed as a replacement for the M29 Weasel for the USMC. This was a lightweight tracked amphibious vehicle with an aluminum body. It could carry cargo or eight marines. The M76 top speeds were 30 mph (50 km/h) on land and 5.3 knots (10 km/h) in water. The M76 was armed with a Browning M2HB 50 caliber (12.7 mm) machine gun. The first 33 vehicles arrived in Danang in 1965. Photographs show a M76 on the Khe Sahn military base in 1968.

3.4
Trucks and Jeeps

Land Rover

The Land Rover was launched in 1948 by British company Rover as a vehicle for agricultural use and was a cross between a jeep and a tractor. It had a steel box chassis and an aluminum body. There were long and short wheelbase versions and many body variations. The vehicle was hugely popular and sold round the world. It was particularly popular in Africa, the Middle East, and Australia with 60,000 sold in 1969 alone. Australian forces used Land Rover series 2 and 2A in Vietnam.

M35 2.5 Ton Truck "Deuce & Half"

M35 2½-ton cargo truck was designed for the US Armed Forces but sold to at least 44 countries. Production started in 1950 and continued until 1999. It was nicknamed "Deuce and a Half" just like its predecessor the WWII GMC CCKW 2½-ton 6×6 truck. The M35 Cargo Truck weighed 6 tons unladen and the top speed was 58 mph (93 km/h).

M54 and other M39 Series 5 Ton Trucks

M39 series 5-ton 6×6 truck was a family of heavy tactical trucks built for the US Forces. The most common variant was the M54 cargo truck, but there were numerous variations. The M54 cargo truck weighed 9 tons unladen and the top speed was 52 mph (84 km/h).

M54 Gun Truck "Eve of Destruction", 3D model from BobMack.com, painted by Bob Sanders.

Die Cast Corgi M35 2.5 Ton Truck "Deuce & Half"

M151 Mutt Jeep

Empress Miniatures Mule built and painted by Paul Eaglestone

Gun Trucks

Gun trucks were deployed from 1967 until 1972. Approximately 300 to 400 were built, but there was no standard design. Gun trucks were frequently painted gloss black with bright colored lettering giving the name of the truck. Typical names included "Eve of Destruction," "Ace of Spades," "Deuce is Wild," "Cold Sweat," "Iron Butterfly," and "Pandemonium".

In 1967, US Army Transportation Corps used 200 truck convoys to bring supplies from the coastal ports to bases in the Central Highlands. The 8th Transportation Group, based in Qui Nhon was responsible for delivering supplies to Pleiku via Route 19. Ambushes and other Viet Cong attacks occurred almost daily on Route 19, particularly at the "Devil's Hairpin" in An Khe Pass and "Ambush Alley" below Mang Yang Pass. In response to the Viet Cong attacks, US changed tactics and ran convoys of a 100-truck maximum with a gun truck for every ten transport trucks.

The first gun trucks in 1967 were based on M35 2.5-ton truck with sandbag armor and armed with two M60 machine guns and sometimes an M79 grenade launcher. Later models were based on the larger M39 series 5-ton trucks, and these had two-layer steel armor and a variety of weapons including M60, 50 caliber M2, and XM135 Miniguns. Some trucks were equipped with M55 Quadmount 50 caliber machine guns. Some M39 trucks were fitted with an M113 body.

M151 Mutt Jeep

The M51 Mutt utility truck, ¼-Ton, 4×4 was the successor to the WWII Willys Jeep and Korean War M38 light utility vehicles. The M151 had an integrated body design which offered a little more space than prior jeeps and featured all-around independent suspension with coil springs. It had a payload capacity of 360 kg off-road. The Mutt weighed 1.1 tons unladen, and the top speed was 66 mph (106 km/h). More than 100,000 M151 Mutts were produced from 1959 to 1988, and they were sold to at least 70 countries.

M 274 Mule

The M274 Mule utility truck, ½-Ton, 4X4 was developed for US Armed Forces and was known as the "Mule," "Military Mule," or "Mechanical Mule." It was a 4-wheel drive, gasoline-powered truck/tractor type vehicle that could carry up to 1/2 tons off-road. It was introduced in 1956 and used until the 1980s. The Mule weighed 360 kg unladen and the top speed was 25 mph (40 km/h). The range was 108 miles (170 km). Mules were often used as weapons platforms with M60 light machine guns, a M2 50 caliber machine gun, or a M40 106 mm recoilless rifle.

M422 Mighty Mite (Jeep USMC)

The M422 "Mighty Mite" was a lightweight ¼-ton 4x4 tactical truck, suitable for airlifting and manhandling which was used by the USMC. The M422 was lighter abut more expensive than the M151 Mutt, but could be carried by a Sikorsky H-19 helicopter. However, a few years later, the UH-1 Huey was deployed and could easily lift the heavier Mutt, so the Mighty Mite was no longer needed. A total of 3,900 were built between 1959 and 1962. The Mighty Mite weighed 750 kg unladen and the top speed was 62 mph (100 km/h). The range was 225 miles (362 km).

3.5 Helicopters

H-21 Piasecki Shawnee, "Flying Banana"

The H-31 Shawnee, also called the "Flying Banana," was a tandem rotor helicopter, originally developed for arctic rescue. The H-21 had a maximum loaded weight of 7 tons and had a range of 265 miles (426 km). The maximum operational speed was 127 mph (204 km/h). It could carry 20 soldiers in cold conditions but carried only nine in Vietnam.

The H-21C was deployed to Vietnam in December 1961 with the Army's 8th and 57th Transportation Companies, in support of Army of the Republic of Vietnam troops. They were vulnerable to the North Vietnamese Army and Viet Cong ground forces, who had 50 caliber (12.7 mm) anti-aircraft machine guns. The H-21 remained the U.S. Army's helicopter workhorse in Vietnam until 1964 when it was replaced with the Bell UH-1 Huey. In 1965, the Boeing CH-47 Chinook was deployed to Vietnam.

H-34 Sikorsky

The Sikorsky H-34 (company designation S-58) was a piston-engine military helicopter originally designed as an anti-submarine warfare (ASW) aircraft for the US Navy. The design was licensed to Britain as Westland Wessex and had a turboshaft engine. A total of 1,881 were built. The US Army did not deploy the H-34 to Vietnam, but they saw extensive service as a utility helicopter for the USMC. The H-34 had a maximum loaded weight of 6 tons and had a range of 190 miles (310 km). The maximum operational speed was 122 mph (196 km/h).

UH-1 Huey helicopter built and painted by Paul Eaglestone

UH-1 Iroquois, "Huey"

The Bell UH-1 Iroquois, commonly known as "Huey," was a utility military helicopter powered by a single turboshaft engine, with two-bladed main and tail rotors. The UH-1 was the first turbine-powered helicopter produced for the US military,

The UH-1 first saw service in combat operations in Vietnam in 1962. These gunship UH-1s were commonly referred to as "Frogs" or "Hogs" if they carried rockets, and "Cobras" or simply "Guns" if they had guns. UH-1s tasked and configured for troop transport were often called "Slicks" due to an absence of weapons pods. Slicks did have door gunners, but were generally employed in the troop transport and medivac roles. During the war, 7,013 UH-1s served in Vietnam, and 3,305 of them were destroyed.

The UH-1 had a maximum loaded weight of 4.1 tons and had a range of 318 miles (511 km). The maximum operational speed was 127 mph (204 km/h).

OH-6 Cayuse "Loach"

The Hughes OH-6 Cayuse (nicknamed "Loach" after the requirement acronym LOH [light observation helicopter]) was a single-engine light helicopter with a four-bladed main rotor used for personnel transport, escort and attack missions, and observation. The two seat OH-6 had a maximum loaded weight of 1089 kg and had a range of 380 miles (610 km). The maximum operational speed was 150 mph (240 km/h). The OH-6 was deployed in Vietnam beginning in 1966 and replaced the O-1 Bird Dog fixed wing airplane for artillery observation and reconnaissance.

AH-1 Cobra

The Bell AH-1 Cobra, also known as "Huey Cobra" or "Snake," was a two-bladed rotor, single-engine attack helicopter manufactured by Bell Helicopter. It shared the engine, transmission, and rotor system of the Bell UH-1 Iroquois. The AH-1 had a maximum loaded weight of 4.3 tons and had a range of 360 miles (570 km). The maximum operational speed was 220 mph (350 km/h). AH-1s made their first combat kill on September 4, 1967, sinking a sampan boat and killing four Viet Cong. Bell supplied 1,116 AH-1Gs for the US Army between 1967 and 1973, and the Cobras chalked up over a million operational hours in Vietnam. Approximately 300 were lost to combat and accidents during the war.

< Sikorsky H-34 helicopter built and painted by Paul Eaglestone

3.6
Boats

Sampans, Junks, & Fishing Boats

In South Vietnam, the rivers are traditional transport routes. Many people live on or next to rivers. Sampans are small rowing boats which are often used to transport goods and people and to sell goods at river markets. Larger sampans can be used as house boats and fishing boats. The term comes from Chinese and means three planks. Larger sea going wooden cargo vessels are often called junks.

Building & Painting Vietnamese Wooden Boats

Barrage Miniatures is a Spanish company with a large range of resin boats, vehicles, and buildings. The range includes small and large Sampans, fishing boats, an ARVN Yabatu junk, and a SEAL STAB assault boat. These models are available in 1/72 scale for 20 mm figures and 1/56 for 28 mm figures. The models follow historical reference books, photographs, and blueprints. They are designed and modelled by Alf Comps and Barrage Miniatures studio. The boats are 3D printed and then hand finished.

The two small boats are sampans, and the larger one is classed as a five-plank houseboat. These boats are all PU resin casts using resin supplied by Form X. The molds are filled from the waterline.

Clean Up the Resin Casting

The first step is to sand the rough edge on the waterline so that it matches the form of the hull. Next, place a sheet of fine or medium sandpaper on a flat surface and push the boat back and forth so that the base is smooth and flat.

If there are bubbles or hollows, these can be filled with Milliput. In this case, no filling was needed.

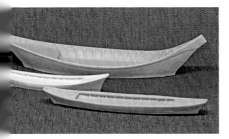
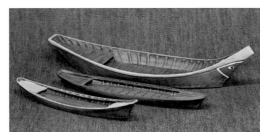

If you wish, you can deepen the wood grain texture by scratching in the direction of the hull planks with a wire brush or coarse sandpaper.

Painting

Once sanding is complete, wash the boat with a little detergent and water. Allow the boat to dry thoroughly. Prime with a suitable spray e.g., Citadel Chaos Black or with brush-on artists acrylic Gesso. Apply a dark brown as the first coat, e.g., Leather Brown 70.871. Create lighter shades by mixing the Leather Brown Tan Earth 70.874. Apply a variety of lighter shades using a damp brushing and dry brushing to achieve an old wood effect. Darken the joints with an application of a very dark brown wash such as Citadel Agrax Earthshade.

The gunwale is a wooden edging along the top of the hull. This is often painted in bright colors, with turquoise and red being particularly common in Vietnam. Paint the gunwale with Light Turquoise 70.840.

It is quite common for larger sampans to have eyes on the bow so that they can see where they are going. Make a simple template by tracing the bow and marking the position of the background and the eyes. Mark the edge of the background on both sides of the bow. Paint the background color, in this case Bloody Red 72.010, and allow it to dry. Next, mark the position of the eyes. Paint the white first and, when this has dried, paint the black pupil. Paint a white outline to complete the face.

Patrol Boat River

Patrol Boat River Mark 2, also known as PBR or "Pibber." This was a 32-foot (9.8 meters) long motorboat used to patrol the Mekong and Saigon Rivers during the Vietnam War from 1966 to 1971. There were about 250 boats on active duty during the period, and they patrolled the rivers and port areas.

The PBR was designed by Willis Slane and Jack Hargrave of Hatteras Yachts, who were famous for sport fishing boats and luxury motor yachts. The glass fiber hull was based on an existing Hatteras Yacht hull. They were powered by two 180 horsepower diesel engines with each driving a Jacuzzi Brothers water pump-jet. The boats reached top speeds of 31 mph (53 km/h). The drives could be pivoted to reverse direction, turn the boat in its own length, or come to a stop from full speed in a few boat lengths.

PBRs had very little armor, but they carried a lot of firepower. The armored front turret contained twin M2HB 50 caliber machine guns. Another M2HB 50 caliber machine gun was mounted on a tripod in the stern. There was also a M60 machine gun and a Mk19 grenade launcher mounted on armor plates behind the cabin. The cabin was lightly armored to protect the coxswain.

In *Apocalypse Now*, a PBR code-named "Street Gang" takes Captain Willard from Saigon to inside Cambodia.

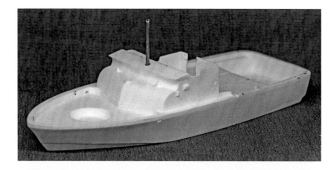

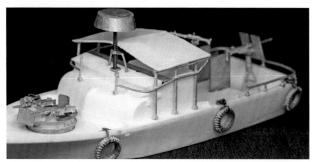

Building the Empress PBR
This Empress model is a very accurate. The model was sculpted by Richard Humble of Fylde Armories. The crew were sculpted by Paul Hicks.

Cleaning
Take a lot of time with the clean-up and dry fit. The model has a polyurethane resin hull and many white metal parts. Sand the hull with emery boards to remove blemishes. If needed fill with Milliput.

Clean up metal parts, remove silver threads from the vents, and trim scabs from the molding gates. The frame for the cabin may have been bent in transit, so carefully bend it back so that the pins match the holes.

Dry Fit All Parts
The handrails have several posts which fit to matching holes in the resin hull. Mark the holes with black spots using marker pen. Clean with a suitable sized drill in a pin-vise. Measure the pins on the white metal parts with a digital vernier caliper and select the matching size of drill bit. Drill by hand with a pin vise drill.

The handrail around the back of boat may have been bent in in transit, so carefully bend it back so the pins match the holes. On the model we received, three holes for the hand-rail and cleat were missing at the port side stern corner (i.e., back left or port). The positions were carefully marked out with a pencil and drilled.

Straighten the canopy as necessary by dropping it into a cup of hot water.

Drill out holes for aerials.

Carefully drill out post for the M60 machine gun, so it is a good fit for the pin which is cast onto the gun.

Wash the resin parts after cleaning up to remove resin dust, swarf, greasy finger marks, and blood before gluing and painting.

Modifications
Replace the radar system pole with a 2 mm diameter brass tube or rod. Drill out the underside of the radar.
Remove rope from tires. Replace with twisted strands of copper wire taken from lighting cable. Make an additional rope for the bow painter.

Making a Base
If you are going to make a base for the model, it is a good idea to plan this now.

Captain Benjamin Willard, Jay "Chef" Hicks, Lance B. Johnson, Tyrone "Mr Clean" Miller, and Chief Phillips from the film Apocalypse Now.

First, cut a rectangle about 250 mm x 80 mm from a sheet of 3 mm thick Perspex. Do not remove the polythene film from either side, as it will protect the surface from scratches during shaping and drilling. Take a sheet of thin card and cut it to the same size as the rectangle. Fold the card to get a center line for the long side. Place the boat on the paper and match the bow and stern to the center line with the bow about 20 mm from one end and the stern about 40 mm from the other end. Draw a line from 15 mm in front of the bow and round to the stern keeping about 15 mm from the upper edge of the hull. Extend the line so that you have a rectangle behind the stern. Fold the card and cut along the line to make a template. Place the template on the Perspex and draw the center line and the outline.

Perspex can be cut with a hacksaw and shaped with a file or sandpaper, but this is laborious. Perspex can be scored and snapped, but this is very unpredictable. The fastest way to shape the Perspex is with a bench mounted disc sander.

Adding Magnets
If you are going to use magnets, this is best done before the white metal parts are attached.

It is nice to have a gaming base and a display base. This can be achieved with rare earth magnets. Round magnets 8 mm diameter x 3 mm have a strong hold.

The magnets should be placed along the center line where the resin is thickest under the front of the cabin and about 30 mm behind the cabin. The positions need to be matched exactly in the base and the hull so use the template and mark the centers of the holes with a 1 mm drill. The Perspex base is 3 mm thick so the lower magnet will sit half in the base and half in the hull. Using a pillar drill and a wood boring bit, drill two 8 mm diameter hole with the flat part the same depth as one and a half magnets – i.e., 4.5 mm. Drill two matching holes 1.5 mm deep in the Perspex base.

A nice feature is to be able to rotate the front turret and at the same time ensure that it will not fall out. To achieve this, fix a 6 mm x 2 mm diameter magnet centrally in the hull under the turret. Using a pillar drill and a wood boring bit, drill a 6 mm diameter hole with the flat part the same depth as the magnet. Glue a 10 mm diameter x 0.5 mm magnet to the underside of the turret.

Assembly
The general idea is to assemble from inside out.

Glue the cleats first. On the PBR Mark 2, the four rope cleats at the bow are set inside the hull below the gunwale. The four rope cleats midships and stern are on top of the gunwale.

PBR from Apocalypse Now with Lieutenant Colonel Kilgore's surfboard.

Attach the search light to the front of the cabin left of the mast.

Attach one of the two armor plates behind the cabin with superglue in the slot. Clamp to an upturned four-pin square Lego brick to ensure the plate dries and sets vertically. Repeat with the second plate.

Attach the tires with 1 mm diameter pins. Replace the rope with copper wire and wrap this around the cleats. Fix the wire with fluid superglue.

Add a painter rope to one of the front cleats.

Attach the search light to the top of the canopy. Fit the flagpole for the Stars & Stripes

Mount the mast with lights facing forward.

Replace aerials with bristle made from stretched sprue.

Assemble the rear 50 caliber machine gun onto its tripod and fix the shield and the ammunition box.

Do not glue in the 50 caliber machine guns on the front turret, as it makes it impossible to mount the gunner. The ammunition belts feed from inside to outside, so right side of the left gun and left side of the right gun. Glue the search light to the pin on the right side of the turret. The cabin frame, canopy, rear handrail, and radar top are all simply dry fitted for spray painting and removed again for weathering. The turret and rear 50 caliber machine gun were spray painted separately.

Painting
Use grey, olive green, or dark green. The correct color was called marine green and is very similar to Vallejo Russian Green. Selected dark olive green similar to the color of one that is in the Museum of the American GI in Texas. The hull beneath the waterline appears to have been red on newly-delivered boats and but later painted black on older boats after maintenance. The canvas canopy was intended to match the boat but faded to a noticeably lighter shade.

http://brownwater-navy.com/

Spray with Citadel Chaos Black as primer.

PBR "Erebus" from Apocalypse Now. The 50 cal is called "Canned Heat."

Spray with Vallejo 28.003 Russian Green Spray. The color is the same as Vallejo 70.894 Camouflage Olive Green (which they used to call Russian Green a few years ago).

Now, the boat looks brand new and very smooth. Overpaint it and weather it to make it look used. The plan is that it looks used, but in good condition like the early part of the film, when they pick Captain Willard up. In the film, the boat is black below the waterline.

Choose whether to paint the boat hull below the waterline red for a new boat or black for an older boat.

Paint the tires with German Dark Grey.

Paint the machine guns with German Dark Grey mixed with silver.

Using silver to highlight the edges of the gunwale to simulate areas where the paint has been scraped off. If you wish, you can also stipple silver to simulate chipped paint. This is easier to do if you remove the handrail and the cabin frame.

Overpaint the deck and gunwale with a mix of 70.894 Camouflage Olive Green and Stone Grey to lighten the horizontal surfaces. Using the same color, paint scratches and patches onto the hull to make it look used.

The canvas canopy looks best faded to a noticeably lighter shade than the boat. Add more stone grey to the mixture above and shade the canvas.

Paint the tires, machine guns, and deck with a black wash, such as Citadel Nuln Oil. This will darken the deep areas to fill black and darken the corners and recesses of the deck. Washes tend to stain some parts that were not so intended. After the black has dried, touch up the deck with the olive-green mix, so the flat surfaces are light olive green again.

The crew and accessories were mounted on 1 mm diameter brass rods. These are added to the boat by simply drilling 1 mm diameter holes in the appropriate places.

Flag
Cut out the flag carefully with scissors. Paint the back with diluted PVA glue and bring the outer corners together. Insert a brass rod and close the flag towards the rod. Twist the brass

Empress Miniatures STAD, painted by Jon Atter.

rod before the glue dries so that it rotates easily and the rod can be moved. While it is still wet bend the flag into an S curve. Remove the flag from the brass rod. Carefully paint the top and bottom of the flag with red and blue to hide the paper edge.

The back of the boat has the name "Erebus" and the 50 caliber machine gun shield has the name "Canned Heat."

Surfboard
Paint the surfboard dark green with a red border. At face height, there is an Air Cavalry patch in yellow and black. Above that is a white scroll in the shape of a quarter doughnut above with black lettering "Lt Col Wm Kilgore." The red border crosses the lower board as a lightning strike and has four curved thorns pointing to the Air Cavalry patch. There is a white diamond manufacturer mark above the lightning strike.

Basing
The boat is attached to the Perspex base with magnets. The first base is intended to show the boat cruising.

The bow wave and twin wakes are made with a small tube of bathroom sealant, Uhu Poly Max Crystal Express. The boat is wrapped in cling film and remounted on the Perspex base. The Poly Max is squeezed out like toothpaste with a thick layer around the bow and two thick stripes at the stern. This is spread around the boat and shaped to form the bow wave and the wakes from the jet nozzles.

SEALs move down the Bassac River in a Seal Team Assault Boat (STAB) in Vietnam, 1967

1st Cavalry Division soldiers ascending hill Operation Thayer II 1967 (US Military)

US 3rd Marines patrolling near Quang Tri River in Vietnam 1967 (US Military)

4 Terrain

This chapter focusses on the landscapes and buildings in Vietnam. There are pictures of landscapes and buildings taken during the conflict. Many techniques are described with tutorials covering vegetation including jungle, grass lands, rice paddies, bamboo, palm trees, and banana trees. Techniques for model buildings are described including resin models, MDF kits, and scratch building using XPS foam. This chapter also shows how to create impressive tabletops such as Hamburger Hill and Hue Citadel.

Terrain will make a wargame look much more attractive. For a quick game at home, a simple cloth table covering with a few trees and buildings is enough to identify the line of sight and obstacles to movement.

If you are going to do several Vietnam wargames, it is worthwhile taking time to build suitable vegetation and buildings. These can also be used for other periods such as WWII in the Pacific. Landscapes carved out of hard foam can recreate natural areas in a realistic manner and certainly look the part for a demonstration game at an exhibition. Hamburger Hill is much more impressive and thought provoking, if the terrain looks like a hill. This can be created using a wooden easel to tilt the wargame table. If you are recreating an historical event, such as the siege of Khe Sanh or the battle of Hue Citadel, then hard foam is the cheapest and easiest way to make realistic buildings.

If you are going to use the terrain in a retail store or at a gaming club, you will want to make sure that it is robust. This usually means a wooden edge to terrain tiles and some plaster coating to protect foam terrain.

4.1
Building the Natural Landscapes of Vietnam

4.1.1 Real World Examples
Vietnam has many different landscapes. On the opposite page are a few photographs from the US military archives showing the variety of landscapes.

4.1.2 Ground Mats
Table cloths and grass mats can simply be placed on a table to provide instant landscaping. Here is a simple home-made mat. The fabric is a heavyweight polyester with a peached (yellowish pink) finish. The cloth is 2 meters long and 150 cm wide. It has been splattered with sand-colored paint and stippled with bright green paint.

More sophisticated textured mats can be made using cloth coated in acrylic bathroom sealant and scattered with sand or sawdust. This can be painted to match miniature bases.

Teddy bear fur can be colored green by soaking in craft paints and then brushing with a pet brush to restore the pile. Teddy bear fur can be a complete table cloth or smaller pieces to represent areas of long grass. Roads and pathways can be created by cutting away the long fur fibers and then applying caulk and sand to created dirt paths.

There are numerous commercial mats with printed ground features on them, and some of them are made from a fleece cloth or even neoprene like a mouse mat.

(Upper) 1st Cavalry Division soldiers ascending hill Operation Thayer II 1967

(Lower) US 3rd Marines patrolling near Quang Tri River in Vietnam 1967

4.1.3 Grass

Grass is an important part of many landscapes. It can be simulated very well with short nylon fibers called static grass. Static grass is made from thin nylon fibers, usually between 2 mm and 12 mm long, which simulate individual blades of grass. In the textile industry these fibers are called flock. Static Grass can be used in different ways to make realistic grass coverage for model landscapes and bases for wargame figures.

Application of Static Grass

Static grass can be applied simply in the same was as scatter materials such as sand and saw-dust. Coat the model ground surface with glue and drop the fiber onto the glued surface from a height of about 55 mm to 75mm. A sieve helps to separate the fibers, so they fall like light gentle snow. Although this simple method works, the results are often messy and disappointing as the fibers point in all directions and the overall effect can be flat and a mess. To make the grass stand vertically, you need to create a static electrical field. The fibers align themselves with the electrical field. This can be done with a balloon that has been rubbed vigorously and then holding it above the static grass.

A much better way is to use an applicator with an ion generator, as this will provide a powerful static electrical field. An electrically conductive glue improves the performance. Water based glues conduct electricity.

Applicators for adding static grass to model terrain consist of an electrical circuit underneath the grass container. This applies a static electrical field to the fibers. The container is covered by a lid with a mesh of holes of a suitable size for the fiber length. A wire from the other end of the ion generator and this ends with an alligator clip. Pins are pushed into the glued surface with the to complete the electrical circuit.

Cheap applicators do not work well, because they do not create a strong enough static electric effect. To make the grass stand vertically, you need a powerful ion generator to create a static electric field with at least 10 kV. Static Grass Applicators with a 9 V battery have a transformer to take the voltage up to 11 kV or even 15 kV. High power professional models generate 20 kV and more.

Choosing Colors

Grass is available in light green shades to simulate spring shoots and medium or dark green for summer grass. Brown shades simulate burnt grass and beige fibers look like dry straw. White grass is used to simulate frosty grass. Manufacturers mix colors to produce blends with names like summer grass, jungle, swamp, autumn, and winter. World War Scenics sell static grass blends in more than 20 different color blends, some of which contain colored foam flowers. Green Stuff World sell their static grass in 12 to 15 color blends.

Choosing Fiber Length

NOCH sell their static grass in 1.5 mm and 2.5 mm for general landscaping and 6 mm and 12 mm for wild sections of long grass. Woodland Scenics sell their static grass in 2 mm, 4 mm, 7 mm, and 12 mm. World War Scenics sell grass at 1 mm, 2 mm, 4 mm, 6mm, 10 mm, and 12 mm. Green Stuff World sell their static grass as 2-3 mm, 4-6 mm and 9-12 mm. The table below shows the length of fibers needed to simulate grass at various scales.

Grass Fiber Length at Various Scales in mm

	1/35	1/56	1/72	1/100	1/150
Man 6 feet tall = 1830 mm	52	33	25	18	12
Tall Grass 2 feet tall = 600 mm	17	11	8	6	4
Long Grass 1 feet tall = 300 mm	9	5	4	3	2.0
Meadow Grass 6 inch tall =150 mm	4	3	2.1	1.5	1.0
Grass 3 inch tall =75 mm	2.1	1.3	1.0	0.8	0.5
Mown Lawn 2 inch tall =50 mm	1.4	0.9	0.7	0.5	0.3

Using a Static Grass Shaker for Landscaping

The applicators for static grass to model landscapes look like a large pepper pot and you use them as a shaker. The World War Scenics Pro Grass Applicator and NOCH Grass Master 3.0 both use a 9 V battery and boost this up to 11 kV for the NOCH and 1.5 kV for World War Scenics. The Woodland Scenics Static King can be used with a battery or an external power supply. All three machines work the same way.

Choosing Glue for Static Grass on Terrain

PVA glue (i.e., white wood glue) can be used for small areas. Better results can be achieved with special glues which dry more slowly. This is particularly important if you are covering a large area. NOCH Grass Glue was specifically designed for the electromagnetic flocking. The NOCH Grass Glue appears to be a PVA with some additives to reduce the drying time.

Method

- Depending on the length of the fibers choose the suitable sized sieve. The NOCH Grass Master 3.0 is supplied with three sieves. The fine 2 mm sieve is for 1.5 mm to 2.5 mm grass. The medium 4 mm sieve is for grass fibers of 2.5 mm to 6 mm length. The coarse 7 mm sieve is for 6 mm to 12 mm long fibers.
- Place the model to be flocked on newspaper or in a tray. This will make it easy to collect the excess fibers afterward.
- Fill the grass container to 2/3 full with static grass.
- Brush some glue onto the area that you want to flock with grass.
- Stick a dressmaking pin or small nail into the glued area. Now attach the alligator clip to the nail.
- Switch on the power and gently shake the applicator over the area covered with glue. The distance should be in the range 12 mm to 75 mm.
- After the glue has dried lift and turnover the model so that the excess fibers drop away. Collect the excess fibers and put them in a container so that you can use them again.

There are a number of ways to make the grass more natural. You can apply different lengths of grass so that there are taller patches. This can be done with handmade card stencils to ensure that only a small area has tall grass. Another technique is to apply short grass and then spray on adhesive and add longer grass in a different color. This technique is called layering and can produce super results.

Static Grass Tufts

Tufts are very popular as a quick method of landscaping bases and scenery. They are available in a multitude of sizes, colors and forms. However, each pack is often US$8.00 or more and it can get expensive. If you want a lot of tufts, it is quite easy to make them yourself.

Tufts are characterized by the static grass stems coming out radially from the glue base giving a realistic hemispherical plant shape.

Gamers Grass sell tufts with fiber lengths of 2 mm, 4-5 mm, 6 mm, and 8-12 mm. Green Stuff World sell tufts in fiber lengths of 2 mm, 6 mm, and 12 mm. NOCH sell tufts with fiber lengths of 6 mm as standard and 9 mm as XL. Woodland Scenics Peel 'n' Place Tufts have 4-6 mm fibers. World War Scenics sell tufts in 17 colors at 2 mm, 4 mm, 6mm, and 10 mm.

Many brands offer a variety of flowers and foliage tufts. Flowers can be made by adding glue to the tips of finished tufts and then sprinkling on sawdust or ground foam in white, yellow, orange, pink, red, blue, or purple. Foliage tufts or bushy tufts are created in the same way using green or brown shades.

Spikey tufts are made in two stages, first make a long fiber tuft and after that is thoroughly dry apply spray glue and short fibers.

Using a Flock Box for Making Tufts

Applicator for Tufts

To make tufts, it is easiest to use a box style applicator. This has identical electronics to the static grass shakers, but in the form of a rectangular box with a metal upper surface. This uses a 9 V battery and boosts this up to 15 kV. The World War Scenics Pro Grass Box Applicator is easy to use and produces great tufts with fibers from 2 mm to 6 mm long.

https://www.World War Scenics.com/product/pro-grass-box-applicator-wws/

Warning: The static grass shakers have plastic housings, so you are protected from the electronic components. This is not the case with a box applicator, as the exposed plate and the alligator clip form the electrical circuit. Make sure that no part of your body is touching the metal plate, the alligator clip, or the foil. Otherwise, you will get a low power but high voltage electric shock. This isn't dangerous, but it will certainly wake you up. Rubber gloves will protect against static shocks.

The process is easier if you make a holder from wood or card. Stick some aluminum foil or a metal strip to the surface to improve electrical conductivity. Make sure that there's a border

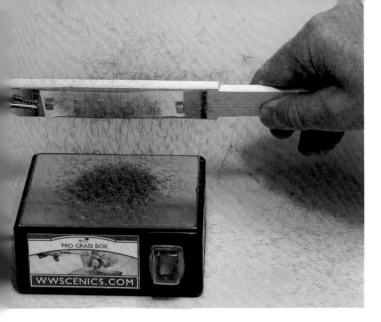

round the foil so that you're less likely to touch the electrical circuit when handling.

Choosing Glue for Tufts

You can use PVA glue or carpet glue. Carpet glue is synthetic latex so dries transparent with a rubbery consistency. Tuft glue needs 48 hours to dry, and, even then, the surface stays tacky. PVA glue dries much quicker, but the tuft base is weaker. From experiments, the carpet glue is significantly better. World War Scenics sells small bottles of carpet glue which is helpfully labelled as Tuft Glue

Method

- Place the applicator on newspaper or in a cardboard tray. This will make it easy to collect the excess fibers afterwards.
- You can mix lengths with 2-3 mm or 4-6 mm, but avoid big differences as they will travel at different speeds. You can also mix colors.
- Pick up about a teaspoonful of static grass and tease out the lumps or pass it through a kitchen sieve to separate the fibers. Place this onto the metal plate.
- Prepare some rectangles of baking parchment or, better still, silicone release paper.
- Clip the paper to the holder. Apply glue spots to the paper. These can be dots or dashes according to the shape that you want to achieve.
- Attach the alligator clip to the card so it touches the metal.
- Hold the card with about 25 mm over the applicator box and switch on the power. The flock will jump from the applicator plate and stick to the glue. Short fibers fly quickly and longer fibers slowly.
- Pass the card back and forth over the applicator until the tufts look suitably bushy.
- Turn off the power and unclip the paper and put it aside. Let the tufts dry for at least 48 hours; sometimes several days in the case of synthetic latex glue.
- Repeat the process with the next paper.
- Once you have finished a batch, collect the excess fibers and put them in a container so that you can use them again.

Adding Leaves and Flowers

To make foliage tufts, use some sawdust type scatter NOCH Leaf Foliage or Forest Floor. Apply a small amount of glue to the tips of the fibers. Take a pinch of the scatter and sprinkle it onto the tufts from about 150 mm above. For best results use two shades of leaves.

To make flowers, use some brightly colored sawdust type scatter such as NOCH Autumn Leaf Foliage or Woodland Scenics Flowers. Just as with the foliage, apply a small amount of glue to the tips of the fibers. Take a pinch of the scatter and sprinkle it onto the tufts from about 150 mm above.

Conclusion

If you are doing large terrain projects or dioramas, it is worth investing in a battery powered static grass applicator to get vertical grass. It is possible to be very creative with different lengths and colors of fibers. With some experimentation and practice, it is possible to make realistic landscapes.

A variety of tufts can be made at home, including grasses, leafy bushes, and flowers. With practice, these can be as good as commercial products. If you need lots of tufts, it can be cheaper to make your own.

4.1.4 Jungle

The simplest way to make jungle scatter terrain is to glue plastic plants to bases made from MDF bases or old CDs. Supermarkets and home furnishing stores often sell plastic plants as home decoration. Many of these end up being offered at reduced prices at end of season sales. Similar plants can be found in aquarium stores. Select plants with small leaves.

1. Dismantle the plastic plants. Here, we see some Ikea plastic house plants.
2. If you use a CD for the base, note that there is a raised circle on the silver side, so this should be upward.
3. Create some mounds so that the terrain is not flat. These mounds will also be used to anchor tall plants. This can be done with carved XPS foam or with air drying clay. In this case, a pre-made mound of air-drying clay was glued onto the CD using hot melt glue.
4. Coat the upper surface with PVA glue and sand was sprinkled on top. You can use other scatter materials such as sawdust, gravel, sand, or ground cork.
5. Paint the ground with medium brown craft paints and let it dry. Afterward, drybrush with sand color.
6. Start with tall planes in the middle. Drill a hole in the mound and glue the stem in place using hot melt glue.
7. Add other plastic plants around the tall plants to create the jungle effect.

4.1.5 Trees

Trees in the Central Highlands of Vietnam look similar to deciduous trees in European and American woodlands. Model railway trees are suitable for wargaming terrain. Seagrass is a good base for realistic trees, but they are far too delicate for wargaming. Model railway trees work much better. Avoid cheap bottle brush style trees with sawdust style flock for leaves, as this tends to shed leaves when handled. NOCH and Woodlands Scenic make trees with clump foam foliage which is more durable. It is possible to add new foliage to repair trees that look bald. Woodland Scenics sell Realistic Tree Kits which include plastic tree armatures and clump foam foliage.

Model railway trees come with bases. If you are using hard foam scenery, it looks better if the trees are pinned to the foam. To do this remove the base, drill a hole and glue in a brass pin. This is not quite as easy as it sounds depending on the material used to make the tree trunk. Bushes can be made from pan scrubs covered with clump foliage.

Tree stumps and fallen trees can be simply twigs collected from garden or woodland. Heat in oven to kill off bugs and fungus before painting.

4.1.6 Palm Trees

Model scale palm trees of various kinds are available on Amazon and eBay. These are sold as Model Coconut Palm Trees 16 cm.

1. Clean up any obvious seam lines on the trunk and remove any flash.
2. Mount the trees on large steel washers. The extra weight in the base will help prevent them from falling over.
3. Make a small hillock of Milliput.
4. Paint the base brown and let it dry.
5. Apply PVA glue to the upper surface.
6. Pour some sand into a plastic tub. Tilt the tub so that the sand gathers at one side. Place the glued hillock in the tub and tilt so that the sand flows over the hillock leaving a coating of sand.
7. Mix the leftover paint with some PVA glue and add water so that it is like a milky coffee. Paint the sand with the mixture and let it dry.
8. Drybrush the sand with a beige highlight color using a cheap pig bristle brush.

4.1.7 Bamboo

Model scale bamboo is available on Amazon and eBay. Search for plastic model bamboo trees. These are nominally 1/75 scale. These are injection molded soft plastic with a soft steel wire core. Bamboo looks good as clumps of about 10 stems mounted on small hillocks of modelling clay. Glorex Keramilight is a cheap and safe air-drying clay which is sold as a soft white brick weighing 125 grams. The texture is like Play Dough. Alternatively, Milliput can be used. Milliput is much stronger but more expensive and needs mixing.

1. **Cut to various lengths.** The stems are all 13 cm long. To create more variety, take 10 stems and keep three at the full 13 cm length; cut five from the bottom so that they vary between 9 and 11 cm; and cut 4 cm from the top of the last two so that you have a short leafy shoot and a 9 cm long stem.

2. **Make Clay Bases.** Slice the Keramilight block into ten equally sized pieces and work each into a ball. Press the clay into a small hillock about 60 mm diameter and 10 mm high. Vary the shape so that some are round and some are ovals. Allow this to dry thoroughly, which many take up to 72 hours in winter.

3. **Drill Holes.** Select a drill to match the stem diameter e.g., 1.6 mm. Drill holes in an equidistant pattern about 12 mm apart so that they form an inner and an outer ring. Assemble the stems to check the layout.

4. **Paint Base Brown.** Remove the stems, paint the base brown, and let it dry.

5. **Add Sand.** Cut some cocktail sticks in half. Insert them in the drilled holes. Mix PVA glue and brown paint and paint this onto the upper surface. Pour some sand into a plastic tub. Tilt the tub so that the sand gathers at one side. Place the glue hillock in the tub and tilt so that the sand flows over the hillock leaving a coating of sand. Remove the hillock and let it dry. Mix the leftover paint with some PVA glue and add water so that it is like a milky coffee. Paint the sand with the mixture and let it dry. Drybrush the sand with a beige highlight color using a cheap pig bristle brush.

6. **Assembly.** Once everything is dry, reassemble the stems and glue them in place.

Real bamboo
(Michael Farnworth)

4.1.8 Banana Trees

Banana tree trunks are very common and distinctive. There are many different species. Most are about 2-3 meters tall and the leaves are over 2 meters long. Model banana trees are difficult to find. There is a plastic kit by Pegasus, but it appears to be out of production.

It is easy to make banana trees with seven paper leaves and a plastic straw as the trunk. For best results, use green paper for the leaves and brown paper to cover the trunk.

1. In 1/50 scale the trunk is 45 mm x 4.5 mm diameter. This can be a plastic drinking straw or plasticard tube. Cut some thin paper and coat one side with PVA glue. Wrap it round the trunk to simulate the bark.
2. The trunk can be fitted with a pin if you are going to use it with XPS foam terrain, or you can mount it on a base. In this case the a spare woodland scenic tree base was used with a 3 mm diameter plasticard tube.
3. To make the leaves start by cutting rectangles of thin green paper 100 mm x 25 mm. Fold this in half along the long axis to create a center line. Then fold it in half along the short axis this creates an upper and lower half of the leaf.
4. Cut a piece of 1mm diameter brass rod to about 70 mm long to create the midrib and petiole (stalk). Open the paper rectangle and apply glue to one half of the paper. Place the brass on the center line and press the two halves of the leaf together. Press down so that the rib is obvious from the top side. Bend the leaves to form an inverted V cross section.
5. After the glue has dried, cut slashes into the leaves and bend the brass wire into an arc.
6. Assemble the leaves into the trunk. From experiments, seven leaves works well, though you can vary this.
7. Paint the trunk in light brown with a dark wash to emphasize the bark. Paint the leaves bright green. Some leaves can be partly yellow, particularly those with many slashes.

4.1.9 Rice Paddies

Rice Paddies are man-made ponds used to grow rice. In flat lowland areas, these are often rectangular but on sloping hillsides, they form complex curved terraces. Each paddy will produce two crops of rice per year. Rice seeds are germinated in nursery beds and then transplanted after a month, when they are about 15 cm tall. They are planted in lines that are about 30 cm apart, and each plant is at least 10 cm apart. For the first three months, the plants are grown in wet conditions until they reach 40 cm tall. Then, the water is drained away so that the seeds ripen ready for harvest. As the rice is harvested, some is retained to provide seeds for the next crop. Water buffalo are used to plough and turn the mud to prepare for the next planting. To spread out the work, the planting is staggered over a few weeks, so at any one time the paddies will be in different stages of growth.

Rice paddies can be made using MDF as the base, but this version uses 3mm thick Perspex.

1. Draw out the shape of the paddies on a sheet of Perspex. Cut it to size by scoring straight lines and then snapping the Perspex. Then sand the edges to make rounded corners.
2. Spray the upper surface with two coats of gloss varnish and let it dry thoroughly.
3. Make long sections of raised pathways using carved XPS foam or foam core. These should be trapezoidal in cross section. For 28 mm figures make them about 3 mm high, 20 mm wide and 25 mm wide at the bottom. These should vary slightly, so that they look natural.
4. Glue the pathways in place with hot melt glue. Miter the corner joints.
5. Paint the base brown and let it dry.
6. Place the paddy fields on a large sheet of newspaper. Paint the upper surface of the paths with PVA glue. Pour sand onto the glued sections.
7. Mix the leftover paint with some PVA glue and add water, so that it is like a milky coffee. Paint the sand with the mixture and let it dry.
8. Drybrush the sand with a beige highlight color using a cheap pig bristle brush.
9. If you are ambitious, you can paint some fish or a snake on the underside of the Perspex.
10. Paint the underside in dark green or coffee brown to simulate the water.
11. Glue a thin sheet of card to the underside to protect the paint from getting scratched.
12. Add tufts in rows.

4.1.10 Rivers

Rivers can be made as solid sections using MDF or Perspex as described in the rice paddies section. Alternatively, using canvas as a base, add two layers of acrylic caulk mixed with paint and cover with two layers of transparent rubber. A very quick wide river can be created using two layers of cellophane on top of a painted piece of fabric or hardboard.

The rivers in 3.6 Boats (page 114) are glossy transparent plastic table covering with acrylic paint on the underside. These are held down to the wargame table with masking tape, and the river edges are covered with teddy bear fur grass or scatter terrain.

4.1.11 XPS Foam Landscaping

XPS foam (extruded polystyrene foam) has many names. Some modelers call it balsa foam while others refer to it as blue foam or pink foam according to the commonly available color in their country. XPS is much stronger than normal white expanded polystyrene foam which easily breaks and crumbles. XPS can be cut to shape with a serrated kitchen knife and sanded to form gentle curves. It can also be cut with a hot wire cutter. Brickwork can simply be drawn on with a ballpoint pen. The pen presses into the foam engraving detail as you draw. Textured rolling pins can also be used to create large areas of brickwork or paving slabs.

XPS foam is available in building supplies stores and do-it-yourself (DIY) centers. It is sold for household insulation and is offered in sheets that are about 1200 mm x 600 mm (4 feet x 2 feet) and in a variety of thicknesses from about 20 mm (¾ inch) up to 100 mm (4 inches). You can sometimes buy XPS in a model store but it can be at five times the price of a DIY center.

XPS Foam Hill

A small hill is an easy project to start with XPS. It is usually better to work with XPS foam that is 20 mm to 25 mm thick. This tends to have less waste than carving out thicker foam. It is also much easier to cut. Thicker pieces can be made by laminating layers. Also trenches and foxholes are easy to cut through just one layer. Use barbeque skewers to hold the structure together and only glue the layers together when the carving is complete.

Simply use a serrated kitchen knife or a small saw to cut out a rounded shape from a sheet of XPS foam. Bevel the edges to create the desired slope. Once the shape is roughly carved, it can be smoothed and blended either by sanding, coating with plaster, or coating with a layer of papier-mâché.

A hot wire cutter is better than knives or saws, because you do not create sawdust. You can buy a cheap battery powered hot wire cutter, but these are not very powerful. A plug-in freehand hot wire cutter with the ability to adjust the voltage is a very powerful and effective tool. This will enable you to work quickly.

Foam can be glued together with PVA white woodworking glue, but this takes quite a long time to dry. There are special glues for XPS foam, but they also take a long time to dry. The fastest way to glue parts together is with hot melt glue. Make sure that the glue is still very hot and press together very firmly, to avoid visible gaps.

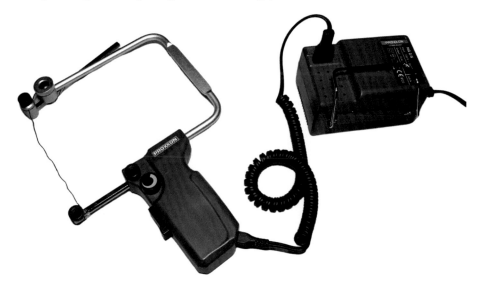

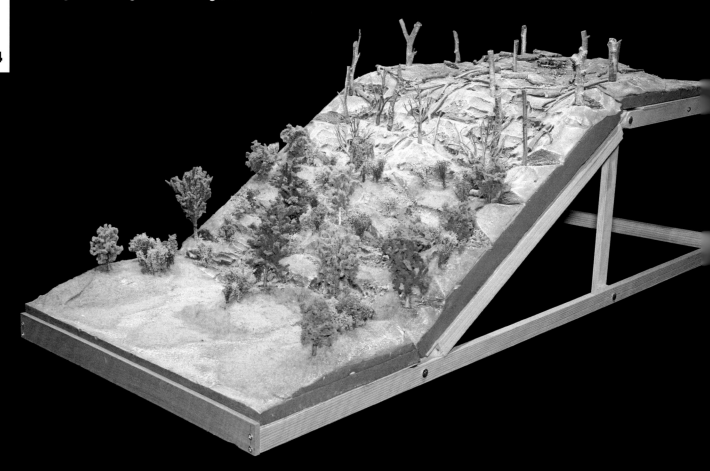

4.1.12 Hamburger Hill

There were several battles in the Vietnam war that took place on steep wooded hillsides. Hamburger Hill is a famous battle that changed the American public opinion about the whole Vietnam War. The story of the battle was made into a film. Recreating this battle would make a very interesting demonstration game for a convention and recall the difficulty that the soldiers faced.

Hills in wargames are usually insignificant. To make an obvious and imposing hill, make a wooden easel which holds XPS tiles.

1. The example framework is a wooden easel which holds three XPS tiles. The entire arrangement is 1200 mm long, 600 mm wide, and 400 mm high. The frame is a simple construction using 28 mm x 13 mm pine bars held together with M5 coach bolts and wing nuts. You can make them using a pillar drill and a crosscut saw. To keep things symmetrical, make matching side bars together in pairs. Drill through two batons and then put a bolt through the hole before you drill the second hole.
2. There is a flat tile at the base, which is 300 mm long. The sloping tile is 550 mm long and the flat top tile is 350 mm long. Later, the three tiles are mounted on thin plywood.
3. The easiest way to make the ridge is to add strips of foam to the tiles. Carve out the ridge and footpaths freehand with a hot wire cutter. Cut the foxholes and trenches with a serrated kitchen knife.
4. Paint the surface with red brown craft paint mixed with PVA glue. Cover everything with sand and ground cork. Broken trees, tree stumps, and logs can all be made from twigs found in local woodlands. Add green flock, static grass, and leaf litter to complete the effect.

Remove the bases from model railway trees and replace them with brass wire pins to stick in the foam. Shrubbery can be made from Green Stuff World shrub tufts mounted onto brass wire pins.

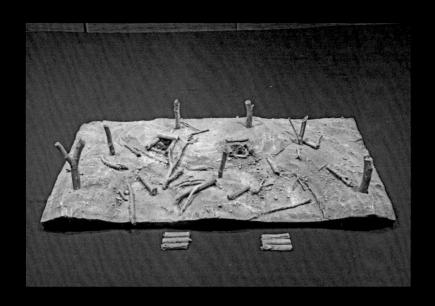

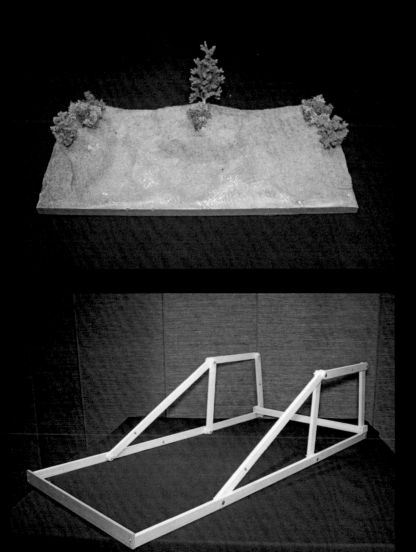

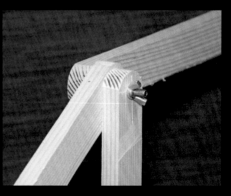

4.2
Making Buildings
for Vietnam

4.2.1 Real World Villages & Cities

Village Huts
(US Military)

*ARVN family housing
in Bien Hoa 1967*
(US Military)

Damaged buildings in Hue during Tet 1968 (US Military)

Long Binh bunker March 1968 (US Military)

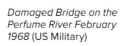

Damaged Bridge on the Perfume River February 1968 (US Military)

4.2.2 Resin Scenery

There are many resin kits for buildings and fortifications. These are beautiful but expensive and need to be carefully handled to prevent damage.

1. Examine the kit and fill in any holes from air bubbles with Milliput or similar.
2. Sand parts to make sure they fit together neatly before gluing.
3. It is usually a good idea to wash resin before painting. Some manufacturers use mold release agents which can cause the paint bond to be weak.
4. Prime with Gesso or an appropriate spray primer. Paint with acrylic paints.

Aquarium Ornaments

Aquarium ornaments are easily available in the form of Buddha statues, Chinese temples, and Angkor Wat style Cambodian temple ruins. Sometimes, these also work for 1/35 or 1/48 scale figures and 28 mm wargame figures.

This Chinese temple scales quite well with a 30 mm tall wargame figure from Empress Miniatures. As the temple is hollow, make a floor by cutting a circle from a sheet of XPS foam. Carve this to fit. Cut or file the surface to create floor tiles. Prime the XPS foam with black Gesso and paint the floor tiles dark grey. Repaint the roof with a reddish color to simulate terracotta roof tiles. Overbrush the steps with dark grey so that the steps and new floor match. The floor does not need to be fixed, as it can be removed so that a figure can be placed in the temple.

In Apocalypse Now, Kurtz's base is an ancient Cambodian Temple with these statues. The originals are in the Guimet Museum in Paris and STL files are available free. The Temple Lions at 65mm tall and the Naga Statue at 70mm tall. (STL for 3D printing)

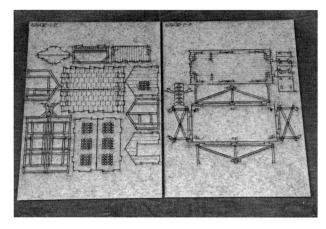

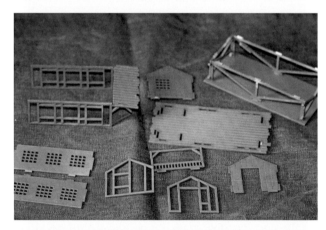

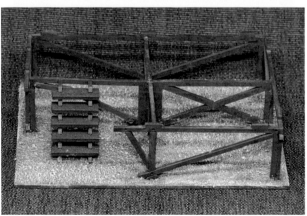

4.2.3 MDF Building Kits

In 2010, a new technology came to the wargaming world. Small CNC laser cutters were becoming affordable and several start-up companies launched MDF kits for buildings, ships, and sometimes vehicles. Sarissa Precision was one of these companies. These kits are typically less than half of the cost of a similarly-sized resin model.

Far East Village Houses

In 2013, Sarissa Precision launched a Far East series of buildings, initially for 28 mm figures (1/56), but later also for 20 mm (1/72) and 15 mm (1/100) figures. The range consists of three houses, each available on low or high platforms, a village meeting building, a watchtower, and a military outpost.

Each kit consists of sheets of MDF that have been cut and etched by the laser machine. The parts are held in place by tiny connectors, where the MDF has not been cut through. Assembly is mostly by tabs and slots secured with PVA glue. However, it is a good idea to dry fit all parts and even dry assemble the whole building before gluing any parts. It is usually best to paint MDF buildings before assembly, so be patient before getting out the glue.

1. **Remove the Parts.** Note the front side has etched detail and the back side have only the cut lines visible. Working from the back, gently press out the parts from the sheet. Apply pressure directly over the attachments. If a part is stuck fast, use a scalpel to release the connectors. Using a small screwdriver or similar tool, push out the squares and rectangles that will become gaps on the final part. It is a good idea to remove all the parts before moving to the next stage.

2. **Clean up the Edges.** Using an emery board or a flat file, remove the remains of the tabs so that the edges are flat. Where there are tabs that go into slots, use an emery board to sand the back edge of the tab to a gentle taper. The joint should go together perfectly flush without any glue and easily separate afterwards.

3. **Build the Platform.** Be careful where you apply pressure when you are assembling parts which have a small cross section. In particular, handle the platform framework with great care. Start with the base and build up the platform. If you do break one of the delicate legs, you can make a splint from photocopy paper and glue it on with PVA glue.

4. **Build the House.** Sand the edges of the house parts to remove the connection marks. Build the house structure onto the platform. Add the framework to the outside of the house.

5. **Build the Roof & Steps.** Build the roof. This consists of two roof panels on two triangular trusses. The roof is designed to be removable, so do not glue it to the house. Build the steps. You will need to sand a slight taper on the underside of every step.

6. **Priming.** Separate the building into sections. Spray with a dark brown color acrylic paint as both primer and color coat. Spray both sides of the MDF, as this will help to prevent warping.

7. **Paint the Colors.** Decide on a color scheme. In this case, the inner walls are stone grey, the outer walls are English Uniform (brown) and the wooden planking is red brown. The planked floors and the wooden frameworks are dry brushed with Leather Brown 70.871 and then highlighted with a light drybrush of Orange Brown 70.981. The inner walls of the room are dry brushed with Stone Grey 70.884. The outer walls were dry brushed with English Uniform 70.921 and then with 50 percent English Uniform and 50 percent Stone Grey.

8. **Build Again without Glue.** After the paint is dry, sand the tabs again to remove the paint. Reassemble the building without glue and touch up the paint as required.

9. **Add Sand to the Base.** Paint the base under the house with Beige Brown 70.875 and let it dry. Apply PVA glue to the upper surface of the base. Place the building in a plastic tray. Sprinkle sand over the base and shake off the excess. Let this dry.

   Mix the leftover paint with some PVA glue and add water so that it is like a milky coffee. Paint the sand with the mixture and let it dry.

   Drybrush the sand with a beige highlight color using a cheap pig bristle brush.

10. **Assemble the Building.** Apply PVA glue to the contact surfaces and the tabs. Push the parts together taking care not to break them. If required, fill visible joints and touch up the paintwork.

11. **Hide the Slots.** In some places, the slots show through on the outside of the building. On the planked sections, cut a strip of paper the same width as the planking and glue this over the slots. Repaint as necessary.

12. **Decorate the Roof.** The roof can be thatched with paper palm leaves or with terry toweling.

   Take a piece of towel and stroke it to flatten the nap. Cut out two rectangles of toweling so that the nap flattens from the ridge to the eaves, Glue the towel with a few spots of superglue on the ridge line. Dilute some PVA glue with water and stipple the towel with the mixture. This will dry to a hard thatch. Paint this in brown shades. When it has dried trim the edges roughly. Leave some trailing threads, as tropical thatch is unkept in comparison to neatly trimmed European thatch. Corrugated card can be applied to simulate a corrugated steel roof. It is also possible to cut paper palm fronds and glue these on to create a thatch.

4.2.4 Scratch Built Buildings & Ruins

Courtyard Wall with Circular Portal

XPS foam (extruded polystyrene foam) has many names. Some modelers call it balsa foam while others refer to it as blue foam or pink foam according to the commonly available color in their country. XPS is much stronger than normal white expanded polystyrene foam which easily breaks and crumbles. XPS can be cut to shape with a kitchen bread knife and sanded to form gentle curves. It can also be cut with a hot wire cutter. Brickwork can simply be drawn on with a ballpoint pen. The pen presses into the foam engraving detail as you draw. Textured rolling pins can also be used to create large areas of brickwork or paving slabs.

This wall is inspired by the courtyard scene in *Full Metal Jacket*.

Cut the wall from a 20 mm thick sheet of XPS. Draw on some brickwork and a circle with a ball point pen.

Plaster parts of the wall with artists fine sand medium texture. After that has dried, cap the wall with corrugated cardboard.

After painting, this is an exceptionally low cost but attractive scenic piece.

Houses

Hoses can be made quite easily with XPS foam. This project is much easier with a hot wire cutter mounted in a table, such as the Proxxon Thermocut 230 E.

The XPS sheets are 125 cm x 60 cm (4 feet x 2 feet) and available in various thicknesses from 20 mm to 100 mm (3/4 inch to 4 inch). It is generally easier to work with sheets about 20 mm thick.

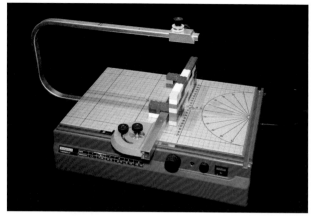

Proxxon Thermocut 230

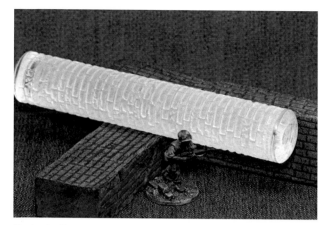

Texture roller

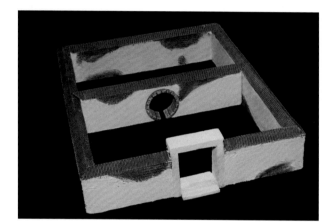

Courtyard

Simple house

House with 3D printed windows and Plasticard roof

Ruined houses

Use a carpenter's trisquare and a ruler to mark out a rectangular slice from the sheet which should be slightly oversize to the final dimension. Cut this with a craft knife and ruler. Then, using the hot wire cutter, take a small shaving off each edge so that you have a nice finish, perpendicular edges, and the correct dimensions.

You can split the foam into two 10 mm thick pieces which gives more realistic wall thicknesses for your houses.

Simple houses need two rectangular sides and two taller rectangles to form the roof. Start by making a rough sketch on paper or card so that you can check the proportions. Then use a figure to work out the height of the doors and the height of each floor. If you are making a two-story house, do not forget to allow for the floor thickness.

It is often easier to make a cardboard template, if the shape is complicated.

Doors and windows can be cut out with the hot wire cutter or with a scalpel. It is sometimes easier to slice the house side into small pieces and reassemble it with gaps for the windows and doorways.

Texture the walls with Green Stuff Roller "Dutch Bricks." Roll the rolling pin over the foam with enough pressure to create a deep and even texture. You can add further texture by spreading artists texture medium on the outside of the walls. Fine sand texture paste creates smooth rendering. Coarse sand texture paste dries to create a textured rendering and is also a very tough outer coating. If you texture the walls with the brick roller and then coat bout 80 percent with coarse sand texture, you get a slightly dilapidated effect of the rendering falling off.

You can add doors and window frames to improve the look of your houses. These can be made from balsa wood or be bought such as Lego windows. If you have a 3D printer, you can print doors and windows to the sizes that you need.

Roofs can be tiled with corrugated cardboard or with vacuum formed plasticard.

Ruined houses are created in the same way. As the interior is visible, use balsa wood or coffee stirrers to create floorboards and roof beams. The rubble sections can be wine corks that have been chopped up in a Nutribullet. Balsa wood and Pegasus bricks may be added.

4.2.5 Hue Citadel

The Battle of Huế Citadel started on January 31, 1968. This battle had some of the fiercest fighting of the entire Tet Offensive. The outer citadel is a 2 km by 2 km walled area, next to the Pearl River, which houses the royal palace and old city center. Inside the main walls there is the Royal Citadel and inside that the Forbidden Citadel which housed the royal family.

More than 5,000 NVA and Viet Cong occupied the city on the first day of the Tet Offensive. The three tiers of Hue Citadel were constructed with earth and thick red brick walls which made excellent defensive positions. The North Vietnamese took full advantage of the defenses and fighting continued until February 25, 1968. U.S. Army photographer John Olsen was assigned to the siege, and his photos became iconic.

The entire structure is made from XPS foam. It is 120 cm (4 feet) wide and 31 cm (1 foot) front to back. The tower is 35 cm tall. Everything is interlocking so it can be pulled apart for storage. Although this looks complicated, it is mostly made up of rectangles and triangles. The main walls and towers and the ground are made from XPS foam 20 mm thick

Step by Step

1. **Make a Design.** First sketch the construction on paper. Study photographs and Google Street View to work out the actual dimensions. Make a few simple card rectangles to check that the proportions look right. Compare these with your figures to check that the scale is about right.

2. **Work out the Dimensions.** It is a good idea to draw the whole thing full size so that you can define the heights of walls etc before you start to cut the XPS foam. From this make a table of key dimensions.

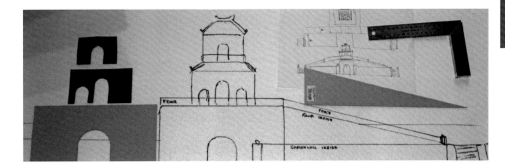

3. **Cutting.** This project is much easier with a hot wire cutter mounted in a table. The example uses the Proxxon Thermocut 230 E. The XPS sheets are 125 cm x 60 cm. Use a carpenter's trisquare and a ruler to mark out a slice from the sheet which is slightly oversize to the final dimension. Cut this with a craft knife and ruler. Then, using the hot wire cutter, take a small shaving off each edge so that you have a nice finish, perpendicular edges, and the correct dimensions.

4. **Arches.** To make the arches, first make a cardboard template and use this to guide the hot wire cutter.

5. **Brick Texture.** Texture the walls with Green Stuff Roller "Dutch Bricks." Roll the rolling pin over the foam with enough pressure to create a deep and even texture. This can be done freehand, or you can make a simple wooden jig so that you have a perfect straight edge. Remember to texture the tops of walls and the insides of the arches.

6. **Assembly.** Assemble parts using clamps and elastic bands. Adjust as necessary before gluing together. Hot glue is a very quick way to assemble but be careful to push the surfaces firmly together or you will have obvious gaps. PVA glue will give a gap free joint but needs to be clamped for at least an hour.

7. **Storage Solutions.** If you want to make a large object easy to store and transport, make tab and slot joints on the underside. Cut long strips and glue them together then slice into short lengths to make the slotted posts. This ensures that the floor height is even all round.

8. **Painting the Bricks.** Paint the brickwork with a dark brown (burnt umber) craft paint straight from the tube. Use a round pig bristle stenciling brush and paint with horizontal and vertical strokes to make sure that the paint gets into the gaps in the brickwork.

   After the dark brown has dried, overbrush with red (red oxide) and then terracotta. Use a 25 mm wide soft decorator's brush. Put a large blob of paint on a newspaper and brush it back and forth. Paint at a very shallow angle, diagonal to the bricks, so the paint only touches the outer texture.

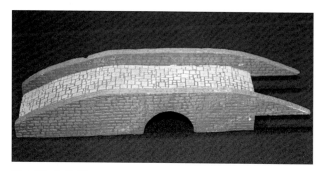

Hue Citadel bridge

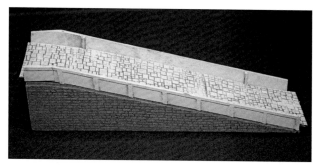

Hue Citadel ramp

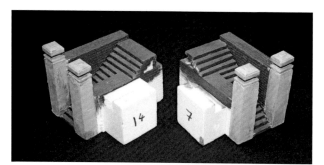

Hue Citadel stairs

Hue Citadel tower lower part

Hue Citadel ground left underside

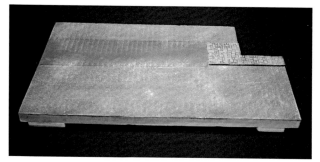

Hue Citadel ground right

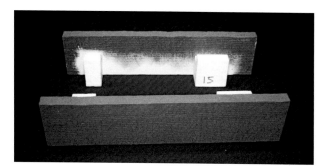

Hue Citadel inner wall

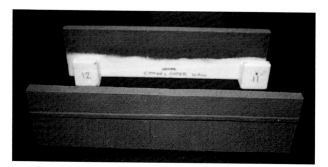

Hue Citadel outer wall

TABLE OF KEY DIMENSIONS

Hue Citadel tower

Hue Citadel gate tunnel

Hue Citadel tunnel walls

Hue Citadel Gate	Metres	1/56 Scale in mm
Citadel inner land height	4	71
Citadel outer wall height	6	107
Citadel wall length	26.6	475
Gate depth	12	214
Gate road tunnel height	4	71
Gate road tunnel width	4	71
Gate wall fence top height	8	143
Gate wall land height	7	125
Gate width	14	250
Ground to top of tower	16	286
Inside wall height	5	89
Ramp width	3	54
Step depth	0.3	5
Step height	0.2	4
Step width	2	36
Table width	67.2	1,200
Tower Tier 1 height	4	71
Tower Tier 1 width	8	143
Tower Tier 2 height	4	71
Tower Tier 2 width	4	71
USMC soldier height	1.8	32

9. **Grey Fences.** Cut the grey fences from 2 mm artboard and add details with strips of 1 mm artboard. Attach these with staves cut from 3 mm square plastic rod. Drill holes and then push the staves in place. These can be removed to simulate battle damage.

10. **Rendering.** The gate and tower are covered in rendering, but this is old and much of it has flaked off. Apply artist's fine sand texture paste with a small trowel.

*US Fire Base made
using resin pieces from
Empress Miniatures*

4.2.6 Bunkers & Military Emplacements

The Free World Forces built hundreds of sandbagged bunkers and defensive positions. Trenches were dug around military compounds and the outside edges were built up with sandbags.

Larger camps often had bulldozers and diggers available. This enabled construction of roads and runways. The earth was bulldozed to created earthwork berms around the camps which acted as defensive walls.

Marston Mats, also called M8 landing mats, are perforated steel planks 10 feet long and 15 inches wide (3000 mm x 380 mm) which interlock to create runways and helipads. Marston Mats were first used in in WWII, especially in the Pacific theatre. A team of combat engineers could build a 5000-foot long runway in two days. In Vietnam, there were problems with plants growing through the perforations and this required frequent mowing. The M8A1 mat was made without holes and was slightly larger at 3,660 mm x 560 mm. Marston mats were also used for roads in camps and as roof beams in bunkers

Bunkers and bomb shelters were also creating by digging out large trenches, so that the final structure was partly underground. Sometimes prefabricated walls were used to create box like structures. Wooden crates and oil drums were filled with earth to make walls. Everything was covered in layers of sandbags.

Sand Bagged Bunker

The Vietnam War style bunker is essentially a hill with a trench that has the addition of a roof and sandbags. Individual sandbags can be made using air drying modelling clay or Milliput epoxy putty. If you require large quantities of sandbags, there are plastic kits from Tamiya and Renedra. In this example, the sandbags have been 3D printed.

There are many resin models of bunkers and trench systems available, but they tend to be quite expensive. Tamiya and Renedra make plastic kits of sandbags that can be assembled to create

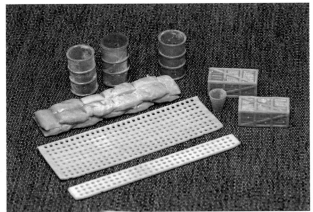

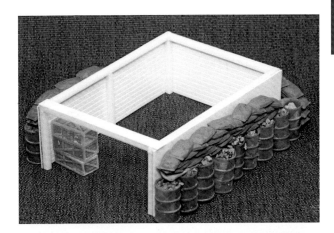

defensive structures. It is possible to make sandbags by hand with Green Stuff or Milliput, but this is very time consuming as the putty has to be mixed. Air drying modelling clay is a bit quicker and much cheaper. However, 3D printing brings new possibilities. Huge quantities of boxes, oil drums, Marston Mats, and sandbags can be printed quickly and cheaply. These can be assembled, as miniature versions of actual bunkers.

The bunker above is based on one at Khe Sanh which was constructed with earth-filled wooden crates and roof beams of Marston Mat. The roof was covered in sandbags.

The bunker based on Khe Sahn is constructed as a plywood box with the side walls protected by earth-filled oil drums and sandbags. The front is constructed with earth-filled wooden crates. The roof is sandbags on top of Marston Mats. There is also a basketball hoop constructed with a wooden post, a plywood rectangle, and a steel bucket.

Earthwork Fortifications
This earthwork fortification represents a small corner of a US military base in Vietnam. This is a 60 cm square with raised earth walls on two sides. This can be placed in a corner of a wargame table. Trenches are cut into the earthworks, and sandbags line the top edges. Each trench can hold five figures to represent a fire team with NCO. The walls include cut out emplacements for AFVs.

4.2.7 Markers & Traps

Often a scenario-based wargame will have hot spots where enemy figures appear or a particular objective such as a helicopter pick up point. These markers are made from plastic wargame bases with laser cut letters and numbers. The bases are covered in sand and decorated with grass tufts.

Bunkers scratch built by Thomas Riepe

Markers for hot spots

Appendices

List of Suppliers

Acrylicos Vallejo   www.acrylicosvallejo.com
s.l. 08800 Vilanoa i la Geltrú Barcelona (Spain)
Tel +34 93 893 60 12 Fax +34 93 893 11 54
Paints, spray paints, texture mediums

Barrage Miniatures   https://www.barrageminiatures.com/
c/Reina Mercedes 22, 4-11
28020 Madrid, Spain
20 mm and 28 mm resin houses, scenic items, and boats for many periods.

Elhiem Ltd   https://www.elhiem.co.uk/
Matthew Hingley
Royal Oak Farm, Bletchley, Market Drayton, Shropshire, TF9 3RZ, United Kingdom
20 mm metal figures including ARVN, Civilians, NVA, Viet Cong, US pilots, and US Army.

Empress Miniatures Ltd   www.empressminiatures.com
Windrush House, Minster Lovell, OX29 ORZ. United Kingdom
Largest range of 28 mm metal figures, resin and metal vehicles, and resin terrain on the
market. All the figures in the range are authentically researched by Paul Eaglestone and
sculpted by Paul Hicks. Ranges includes ARVN, Civilians, NVA, Viet Cong, USMCs, US Army,
Australian and New Zealand Army Corps, Brown water navy, and various special forces.

The range is increasing constantly with a great deal more to be added in the near future.
Empress Miniatures has also taken the trouble to sculpt the different ethnic physiques to
show the accurate size of people.

The range also includes one of the leading sets of rules for the conflict, BOHICA. There are
also packs of character figures from such films as *Apocalypse Now* and *Full Metal Jacket*.
More are to be added. The range also covers the period of the French Indo China War with
French forces and Viet Minh (all of which work for the later US incursion as well.) and there
are plans to increase this range significantly.

Empress Miniatures Ltd has distributors in various countries.
> **Age of Glory USA.**
> **Elite Miniatures Australia,**
> **Atlantica, Spain, EU**
> **Miniaturicum, Germany, EU**
> **Tabletopper, Netherlands, EU**

Full Metal Miniatures   https://www.fullmetalminiatures.com/
The Bombay Crab, 259 Telegraph Road, DEAL, CT14 9EJ, United Kingdom
Large range of 28 mm metal figures including ARVN, Civilians, NVA, Viet Cong, and US Army.
Comprehensive range of metal and resin vehicles.

Games Workshop Ltd   www.games-workshop.com
Willow Rd, Lenton, Nottingham, NG7 2WS, United Kingdom
Large company specializing in fantasy and science fiction games, which also offers paints,
basing materials, and tools.

Green Stuff World International www.greenstuffworld.com/en
Calle Espronceda 10, local 03013, Alicante, Spain
Supplier of sculpting materials, texture rolling pins, tufts, shrubs, snow, leaf punches, and magnets.

Gringo 40s http://www.gringo40s.com/
74 Crofton Road, Orpington, Kent. BR6 8HY. United Kingdom
28 mm metal figures including ARVN, Civilians, NVA, Viet Cong, and US Army.

Italeri
Italian manufacturer of plastic kits including helicopters and AFVs in 1/72, 1/48, and 1/35 scales.

Milliput
Epoxy putty

Noch
German supplier of scenic items for model railways.

Orion
Russian manufacturer of 1/72 scale soft plastic figures including ARVN,
Ruff-Puffs, Viet Cong, and NVA.

Pendraken Miniatures https://www.pendraken.co.uk/
Pendraken, Cleveland House, Webb Road, Skippers Lane Industrial Estate,
Middlesbrough, TS6 6HD, United Kingdom
1/144 scale 12 mm metal figures including NVA, Viet Cong, and US Army.
Comprehensive range of metal vehicles.
USA distributor:
      Dark Horse Hobbies (USA) https://darkhorsehobbies.com/

Proxxon https://www.proxxon.com/en/
PROXXON GmbH, Industriepark Region Trier
Dieselstraße 3 – 7, 54343 Föhren, Germany
PROXXON Inc. 130 US Hwy 321 SW Hickory, NC 28602, USA
Model making tools and machines including hot wire cutters.

Revell
German manufacturer of plastic kits including helicopters and AFVs.

Rubicon Models http://www.rubiconmodels.com/index.php
Rubicon USA https://www.rubiconmodelsusa.com/
Rubicon Models UK Ltd
Allanson House, Walley Street, Biddulph, Stoke on Trent, stevep@rubiconmodels.com
Staffordshire, ST86TN, United Kingdom
Large range of plastic kits for figures and vehicles from WWII and Cold War periods. Vietnam range includes ARVN, NVA, Viet Cong, Australians, US Army and USMC. Vehicle kits for M113 in several variants, Centurion, T-54, M48A3, and UH-1 Huey.

Sarissa Precision ltd. www.sarissa-precision.com
Unit 4 Thorpes Road Industrial Estate, Heanor, Derbyshire,
DE75 7EE, United Kingdom
MDF bases, MDF buildings

Star Decals
https://www.star-decals.net/

Johan Lexell, Stockholmsvägen 12 B:, 15240 Södertälje, Sweden.
Water slide decals including Vietnam War vehicles

The Assault Group
https://theassaultgroup.co.uk/

Unit L, Broxtowe Park, Calverton Drive, Nottingham, NG8 6QP, United Kingdom
Large range of 28 mm metal figures including ANZAC, ARVN, Civilians, NVA,
Viet Cong, and US Army. Figures sculpted by Richard Ansell and Sue Wells.
Also 1/56 scale M113 and M113 ACAV.

Warbases
www.warbases.co.uk

86b Main Street, Cairneyhill, Fife, KY12 8QU, United Kingdom
MDF bases, MDF buildings, tufts

Woodland Scenics
American supplier of scenic items for model railways.

World War Scenics
British supplier of scenic items for model railways.

12th Inf, 4th Inf Div, Vietnam
War Hill 530 (US Military)

Resources

Further Reading
The following books were consulted in the preparation of this book and may be of interest to readers:

Army of the Republic of Vietnam 1955-75 Gordon L Rottmann (Osprey Men at Arms 2010)

Armies of the Vietnam War 1962-75, Philip Katcher (Osprey Men at Arms 1980)

Armies of the Vietnam War 2, Lee E Russell (Osprey Men at Arms 1983)

The Battle of Hue 1968 Dr. James H. Willbanks (Osprey Campaign 2021)

Camouflage Uniforms, Martin J Brayley, (Crowood Press 2009). This book has 400 photographs of camouflage uniforms used by the world's militaries from 1940 to 2008.

The French Indochina War 1946-54, Martin Windrow (Osprey Men at Arms 1998)

Soldier: A Visual History of the Fighting Man (Dorling Kindersley 2007). This is a huge coffee table 360-page encyclopedia featuring articles about USMC and Viet Cong guerrillas.

The Vietnam War: The Definitive Illustrated History (Dorling Kindersley 2017). This is a huge coffee table 360-page encyclopedia crammed with photographs which explain the history and describes events, participants, places, and objects.

The War in Cambodia 1970-75, Kenneth Conboy and Kenneth Bowra (Osprey Men at Arms 1989)

The War in Laos 1960-75, Kenneth Conboy (Osprey Men at Arms 1989)

Weapons and Field Gear of the North Vietnamese Army and Viet Cong, Edward J Emering (Schiffer Military History 1998). This is a large format 160-page book full of pictures of uniforms, weapons, and equipment.

Websites

LAF Lead Adventure Forum   www.lead-adventure.de
Lead Adventure is a forum for wargamers and figure painters which has an active membership of hobbyists. This is a good place to see wargames projects and to get tips on techniques and materials.

Facebook Groups
There are many Facebook groups with small communities covering particular wargames periods and rules, 3D printing, foam modeling, and terrain building.

YouTube
YouTube has numerous channels relating to terrain building, including the Terrain Tutor and Geek Gaming.

Wikipedia
Wikipedia has extensive pages devoted to the Vietnam War history and military equipment.

TV Documentary

The Vietnam War
This ten-part television documentary was made in 2017 and is 17 hours long. It was written by Geoffrey C. Ward and directed by Ken Burns and Lynn Novick. It is packed with interviews and newsreel footage. There is also a book to accompany the series.

Films

There are a lot of films which cover aspects of the Vietnam War. Here is a selection of acclaimed and popular films which focus on the combat and military life.

Apocalypse Now
1979 film directed by Francis Ford Coppola. This is part war film and part horror story about a journey upriver into Cambodia to assassinate an insane US colonel who has gone rogue. Includes the iconic Air Cavalry helicopter attack to the tune of "The "Ride of the Valkyries".

Born on the 4th of July
1989 anti-war drama film directed by Oliver Stone based on the autobiography by Ron Kovic. Tom Cruise played Kovic, a US Marine who was paralyzed during the Vietnam War and later became an anti-war activist.

Danger Close
2019 film depicts the battle of Long Tan in August 1966 between a company of ANZACS and the NVA.

Full Metal Jacket
1987 film by Stanley Kubrick. The first half follows the training of US Marines and in the second half they are deployed in the city of Hue during the 1968 Tet Offensive.

Good Morning Vietnam
1987 American comedy-drama war film based on Armed Forces Radio Service DJ Adrian Cronauer. Robin Williams plays the DJ who was based in Saigon in 1965.

Hamburger Hill
1987 film by John Irvin about the horrific ten-day assault of the heavily defended Hill 937 in 1969 by the 101st Airborne.

Platoon
1986 film written and directed by Vietnam veteran, Oliver Stone. The film tells a gritty story of an infantry platoon near to the Cambodian border in 1967 and is based on Oliver Stone's own experiences.

The Deer Hunter
1978 American epic war drama directed by Michael Cimino about a trio of steelworkers whose lives were changed forever after fighting in the Vietnam War. Stars Robert De Niro, Christopher Walken, John Savage, and Meryl Streep. Most of the story takes place in the US.

The Green Berets
1968 film directed and staring John Wayne, with George Takei as a Montagnard captain. The battle is based on Nam Dong, when Green Berets and CIDG soldiers fought of an attack by a much larger VC force in 1964. The film was supported by the US Army shot at Fort Benning and all uniforms, vehicles, aircraft and jingoistic attitudes were real and current.

The Last Full Measure
2019 film about the award of a Medal of Honor to a USAF Pararescue man for a rescue mission on April 11, 1966, at Xa Cam My.

We Were Soldiers
2002 American war film directed by Randall Wallace and starring Mel Gibson. Based on a book of the same name, the film depicts the battle of Ia Drang on November 14, 1965.

Glossary

Agent Orange	Herbicide used to clear jungle areas.
AH-1 Cobra	Attack helicopter
AK47	Soviet designed assault rifle.
ANZAC	Australian & New Zealand Army Corps
APC	Armored personnel carrier
AR15	US designed assault rifle. Predecessor of M16
ARVN	Army of the Republic of Vietnam, i.e., South Vietnamese Army
BTR40	Soviet wheeled APC
BTR-50	Soviet tracked APC
Centurion	British made MBT used by ANZAC forces
CH-47 Chinook	Transport helicopter with two rotors
Khmer Rouge	Cambodian Communist Forces
Land Rover	British made all-terrain vehicle used by ANZAC forces
LRRP	Long range reconnaissance patrol
LVTP-5	Landing Vehicle Tracked Personnel 5. Large amphibious APC used by USMC.
M1 & M2 Carbine	US developed WWII carbine used by ARVN & Korean forces.
M1 Garand	US developed WWII rifle used by ARVN & Korean forces.
M106	M113 tracked APC with 107 mm mortar.
M113 ACAV	Air Cavalry Assault Vehicle. Tracked M113 APC with added gun shields.
M14 Battle Rifle	US designed battle rifle.
M151 Mutt Jeep	All-terrain vehicle used by US & ARVN. Successor to Jeep
M16 Assault Rifle	US designed assault rifle.
M18 Claymore	Anti-personnel mine
M1918 BAR	Browning Automatic Rifle used by ARVN
M1919 Browning 30 Caliber	US designed 30 caliber machine gun used on tripod or mounted on a vehicle.
M1A1 Thompson	US designed SMG
M203 Grenade Launcher	US designed underslung grenade launcher for M16.
M24 Chaffee	US light tank from late WWII, used by French & ARVN.
M274 Mule	Small utility vehicle used by US forces
M2HB Browning 50 Caliber	US designed 50 caliber machine gun used on tripod or mounted on a vehicle.
M35 Truck Deuce & Half	Military truck
M40 Recoilless Rifle	US designed recoilless rifle used by US & ARVN
M40 Rifle	Bolt action sniper rifle
M41 Walker Bulldog	Light Tank used by ARVN.
M42 Duster	US built M48 tank chassis fitted with twin 30 mm auto canon
M422 Mighty Mite	All-terrain vehicle used by USMC. Successor to Jeep
M48 A3 Patton	MBT used by US forces &later by ARVN
M50 Ontos	Small tracked armored vehicle fitted with six recoilless rifles.
M551 Sheridan	Air transportable Light Tank
M577	M113 tracked APC with enlarged cabin used as command vehicle.

M60 Machine Gun	US designed light machine gun used on bipod or mounted on a vehicle.
M67 Zippo	M48 chassis fitted with flame thrower.
M706 Cadillac Gage Commando	Armored car used by US & ARVN.
M72 LAW	US designed single use rocket propelled grenade.
M728	Combat engineer vehicle
M76 Otter	Tracked amphibious vehicle used by USMC
M79 Blooper	US designed grenade launcher.
MACV	Military Area Command Vietnam
MRT	Main battle tank
Napalm	Mix of gasoline & polystyrene used as incendiary
NVA	North Vietnamese Army
OH-6 Loach	Hughes OH-6 Cayuse LOH—Light Observation Helicopter
PAVN	People's Army of Vietnam
PBR Boat	Patrol Boat River
PT76	Soviet designed amphibious light tank.
RPD LMG	Soviet designed light machine gun used on bipod
RPG 7	Soviet designed rocket propelled grenade.
Sagger	Soviet designed anti-tank guided missile. 9M14 Malyutka AT-3 Sagger
Sampan	Small wooden boat common in Asia
SEAL	US Navy Special Forces able to operate from sea, air, or land.
Sikorsky H-34	Helicopter used by USMC
Simonov SKS rifle	Soviet designed battle rifle
SOG	US Special Forces Special Operations Group
Stab Boat	SEAL Team Assault Boat
T-54/T-55	Soviet designed MBT
Type 59	Chinese version of T-55.
UH-1 Huey	US designed helicopter used as gunships, troop transport, & for casualty evacuation.
USMC	United States Marine Corps
Viet Cong	Vietnamese Communist forces in South Vietnam